Sheffield Ontario and Area in Photos, Saving Our History One Photo at a Time

Photography
by Barbara Raué
©2018

Series Name:
Cruising Ontario

Book 45: Sheffield, Kirkwall, Westfield

Cover photo: Sheffield Home

Series Name: Cruising Ontario
Saving Our History One Photo at a Time
in colour photos

Towns in Alphabetical Order:
Aberfoyle, Acton, Alton, Amherstburg, Ancaster, Arthur, Auburn, Aylmer, Ayr, Beaver Valley, Belgrave, Belleville, Bloomingdale, Blyth, Brantford, Brockville, Burford, Burlington, Caledon, Caledonia, Cambridge, Carlow, Chatsworth, Clifford, Collingwood, Conestogo, Delhi, Dorchester to Aylmer, Drayton, Drumbo, Dundas, Dunlop, Eden Mills, Elmira, Elora, Erin, Essex, Fergus, Goderich, Grimsby, Guelph, Hagersville, Hamilton, Hanover, Harriston, Hespeler, Jarvis, Kingston, Kingsville, Kitchener, Lake Superior, Lincoln, Linwood, Listowel, London, Lucknow, Merrickville, Mono, Mount Forest, Mount Pleasant, Neustadt, New Hamburg, Newboro, Newport, Niagara-on-the-Lake, Oakville, Onondaga, Orangeville, Orillia, Owen Sound, Palmerston, Paris, Pelham, Perth, Peterborough, Petrolia, Port Colborne, Port Elgin, Portland, Preston, Rockwood, Sarnia, Sault Ste. Marie, Seaforth, Sheffield, Shelburne, Simcoe, Smiths Falls, Smithville, Southampton, St. Catharines, St. George, St. Jacobs, St. Marys, St. Thomas, Stoney Creek, Stratford, Thamesford, Thunder Bay, Tillsonburg, Toronto, Waterdown, Waterford, Waterloo, Welland, Wellesley, Westport, Windsor, Wingham, Woodstock

Book 196: Pelham
Book 197: Beaver Valley
Book 198: Chatsworth
Book 199: Wingham

Other Books by Barbara Raue

Coins of Gold

Arrows, Indians and Love

The Life and Times of Barbara
Volume 1: Inventions That Have Enhanced My Life
Volume 2: Entertainment That I Have Enjoyed
Volume 3: East Coast Trips
Volume 4: Olympics Have Always Intrigued Me
Volume 5: Wonders of the World
Volume 6: Caribbean Cruises We Have Enjoyed
Volume 7: Animals
Volume 8: Storms and Other Major Disasters in My Lifetime
Volume 9: Wars, Terrorist Attacks and Major Disasters

The Cromwell Family Book

Laura Secord Discovered

Daddy Where Are You?

Montana Series
Book 1: Montana Dream
Book 2: Life on the Montana Frontier
Book 3: Montana to Boston and Back
Book 4: Montana Sons Go to War
Book 5: Montana Sons Return From War

Visit Barbara's website to view all of her books
http://barbararaue.ca

Sheffield

Sheffield, located 35 kilometres from the city core, is part of the municipality of Hamilton. Sheffield was settled by the early 1800s and the village was founded by Reverend John A. Cornell who emigrated from Dutchess County, New York in 1809. In 1834 he built the first local church on the site where the United Church is now located.

Kirkwall

Kirkwall is located about 13 kilometres east of Cambridge.

Westfield Heritage Village

Westfield Heritage Village is located at 1049 Kirkwall Road off Highway 8 west of Rockton. It has over thirty historical buildings which have been restored.

© 2018 by Barbara Raue - All the photos in this book have been taken with my cameras. I own the rights to them.

Sheffield Homes and Barns

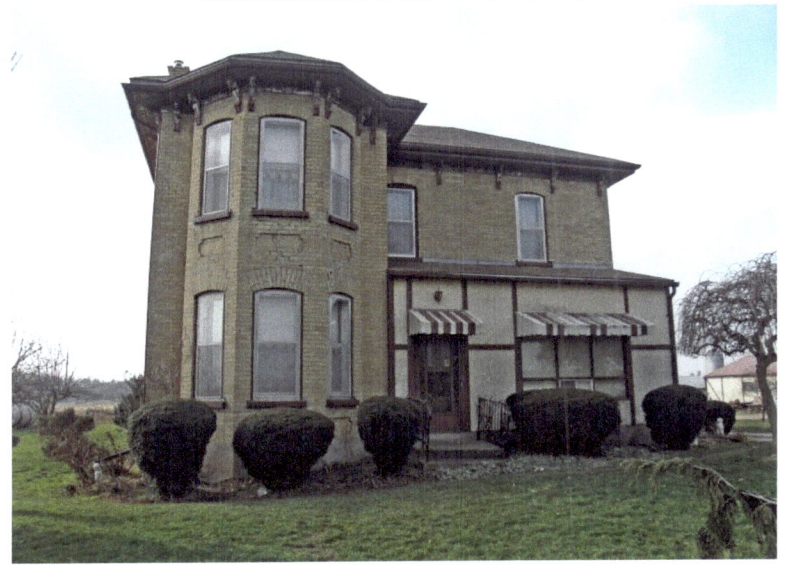

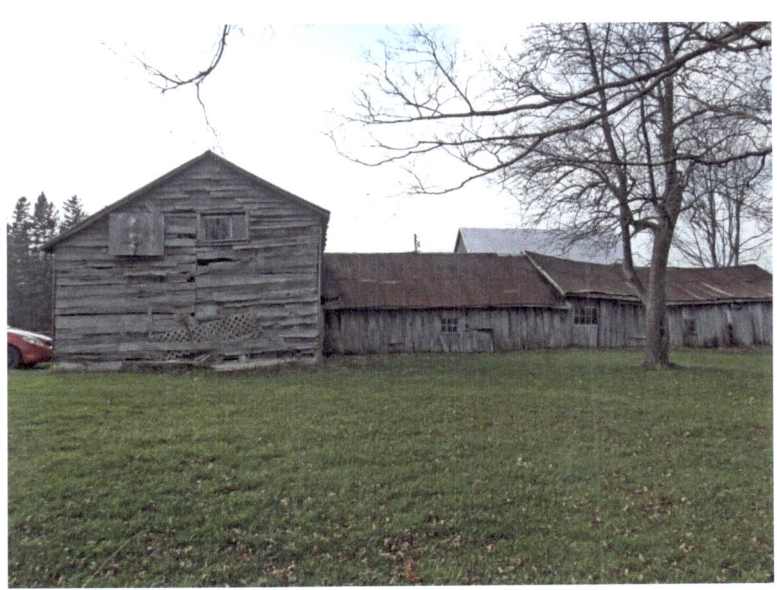

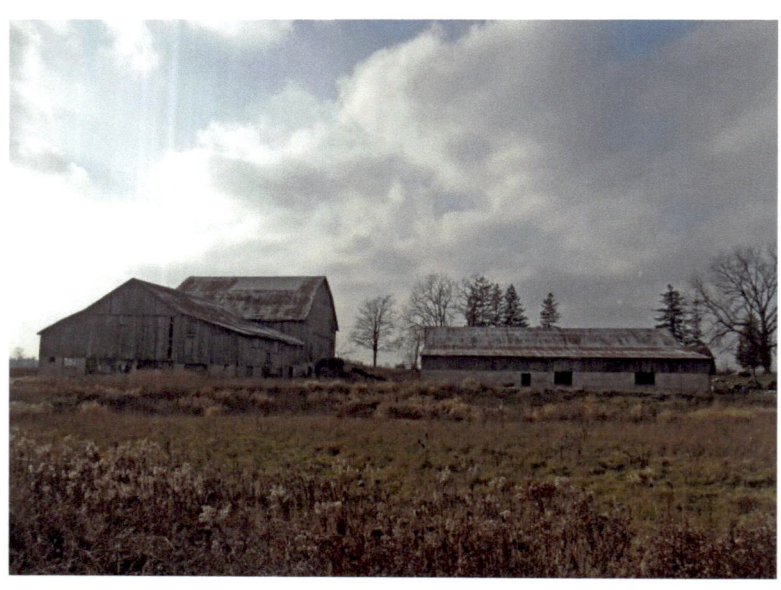

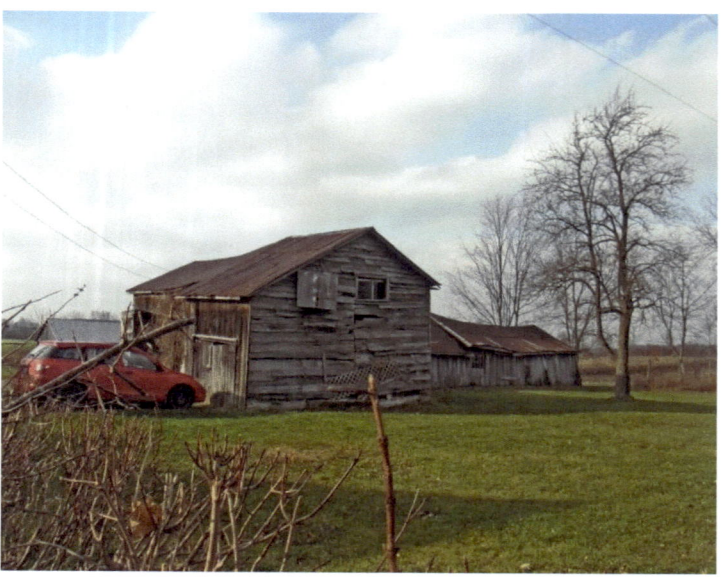

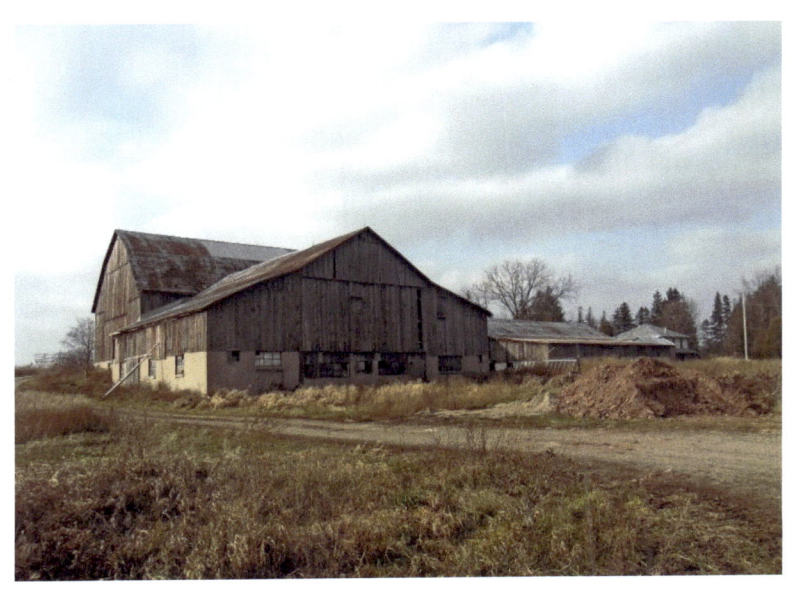

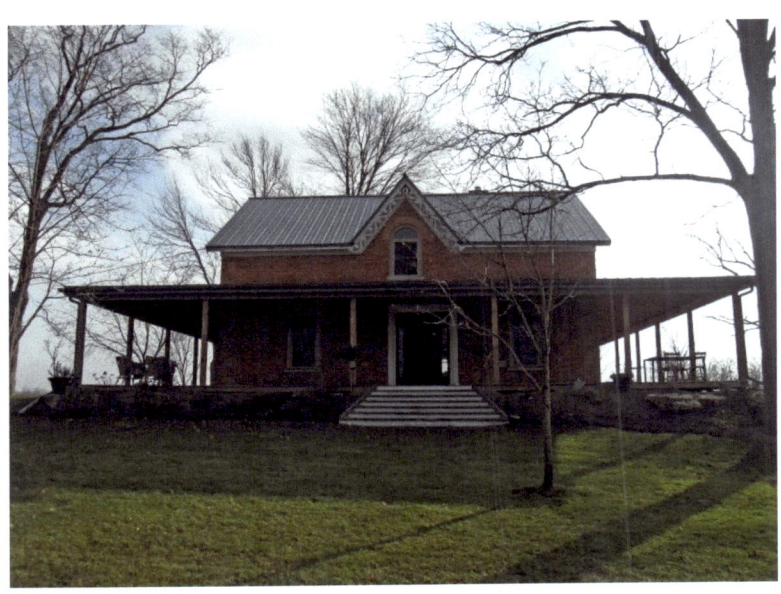

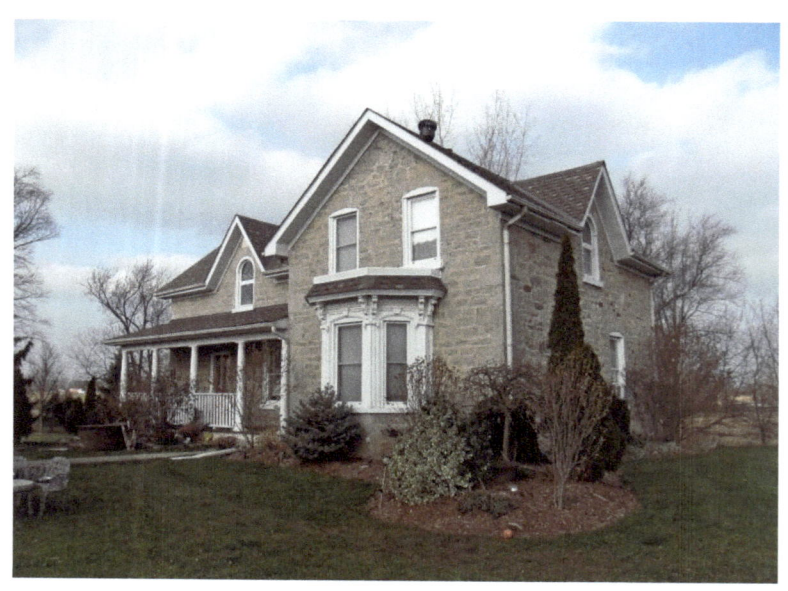

908 Settlers Road - stone house A.D. 1884

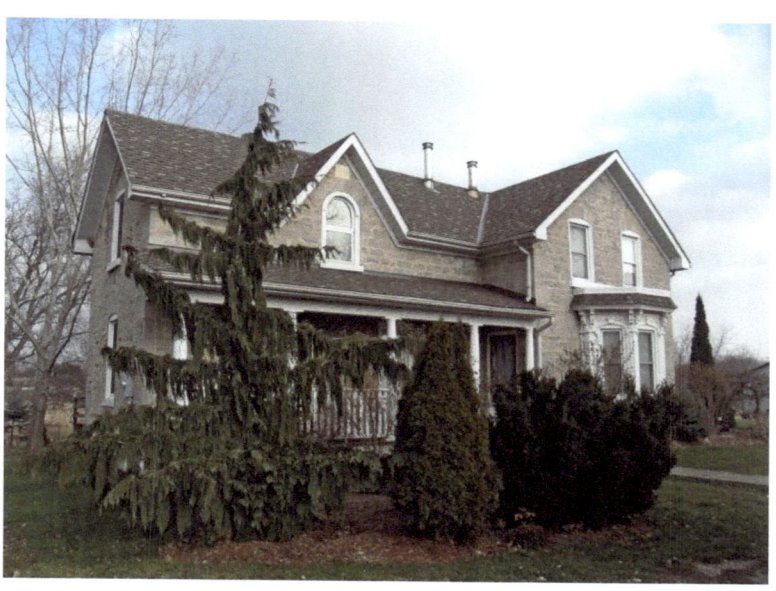

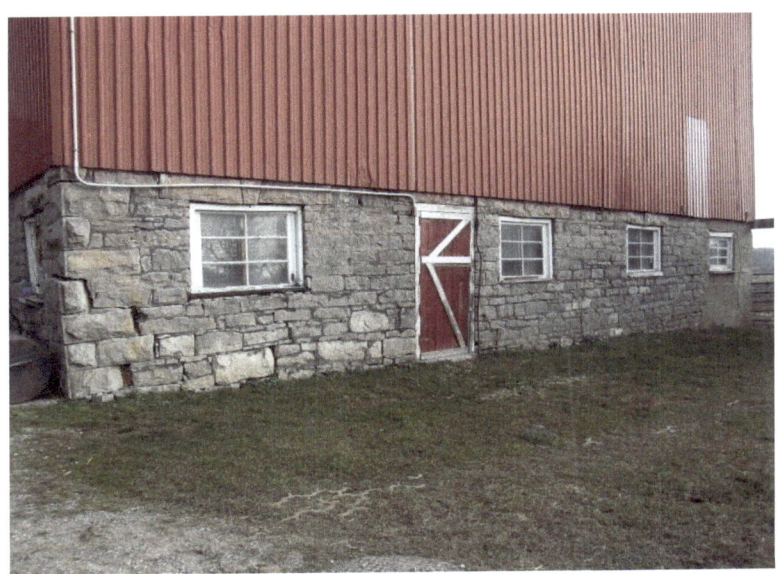
Limestone block foundation and lower wall of barn

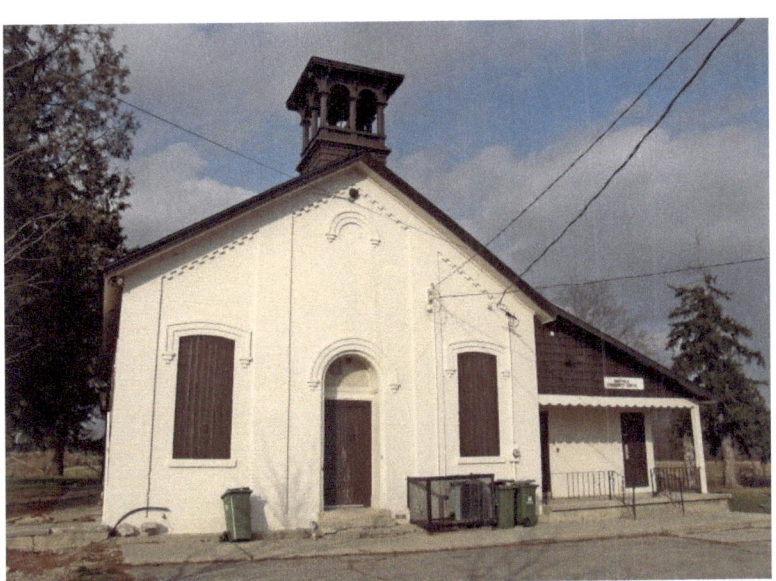
School Section No. 9 – 1877 – Sheffield Community Centre

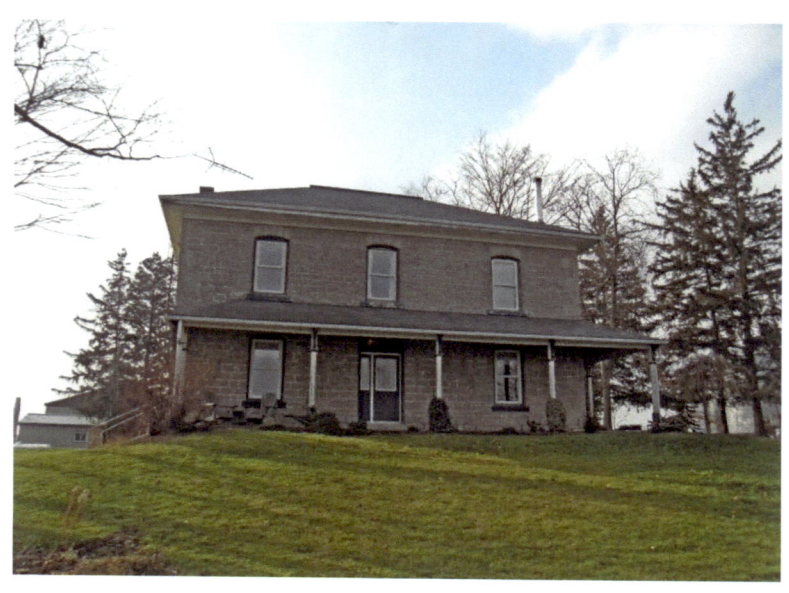

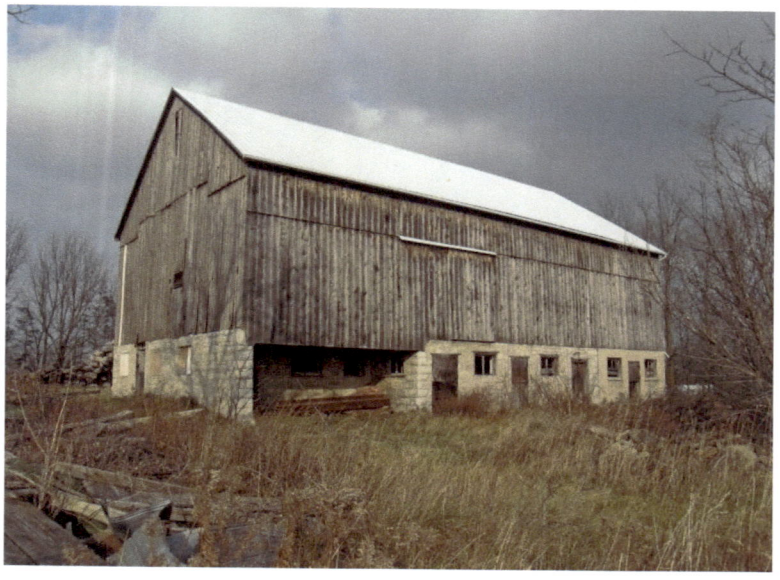

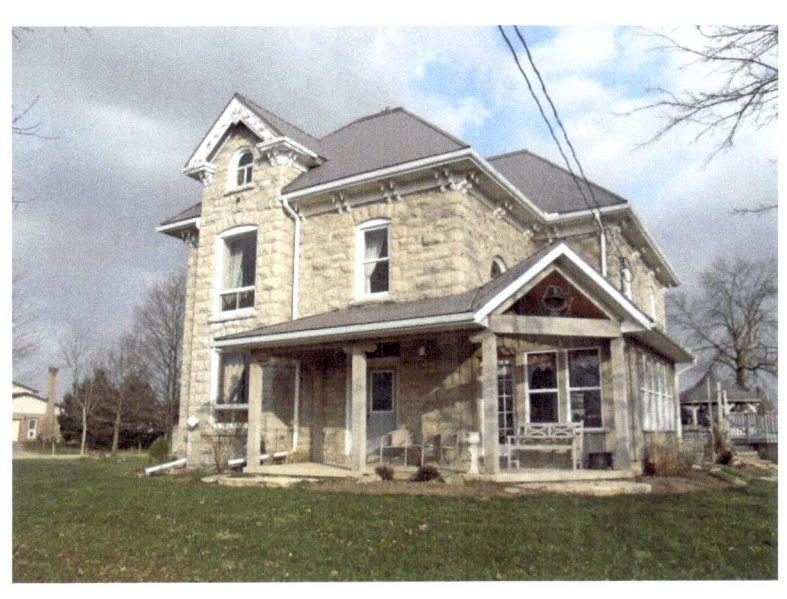

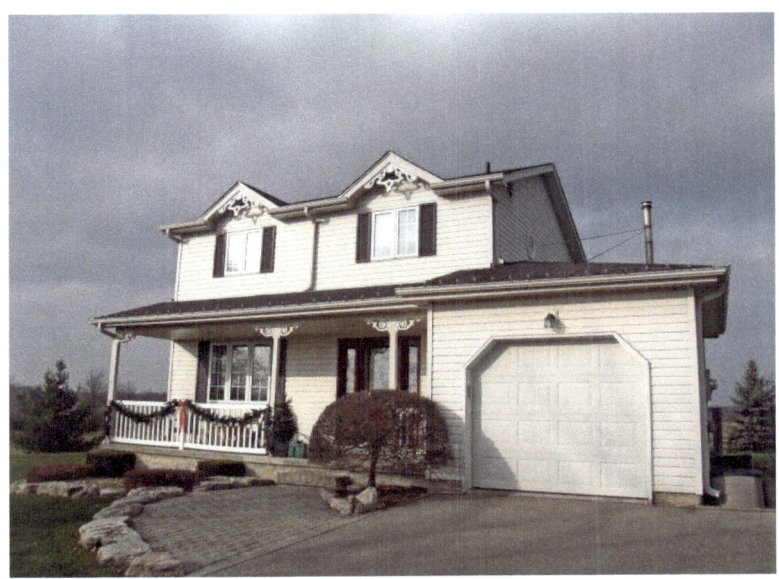

2359 Concession Six West

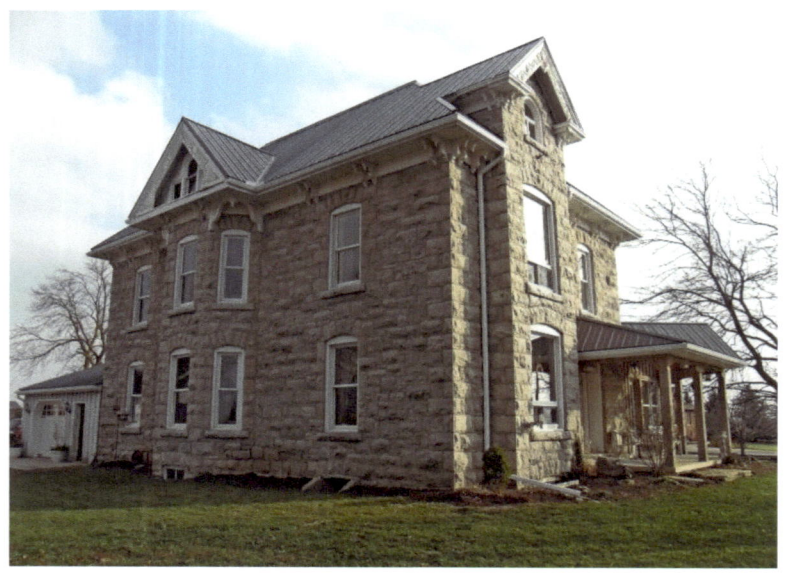

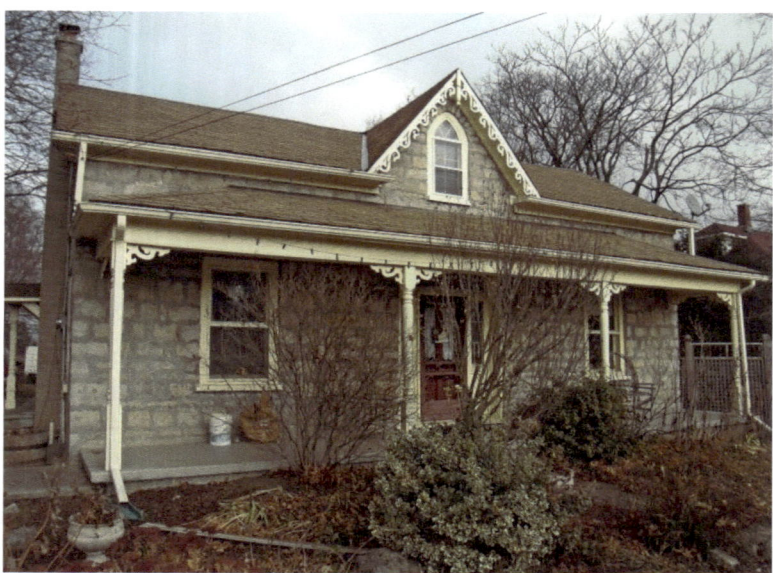

Gothic Style centre arch with gingerbread trim

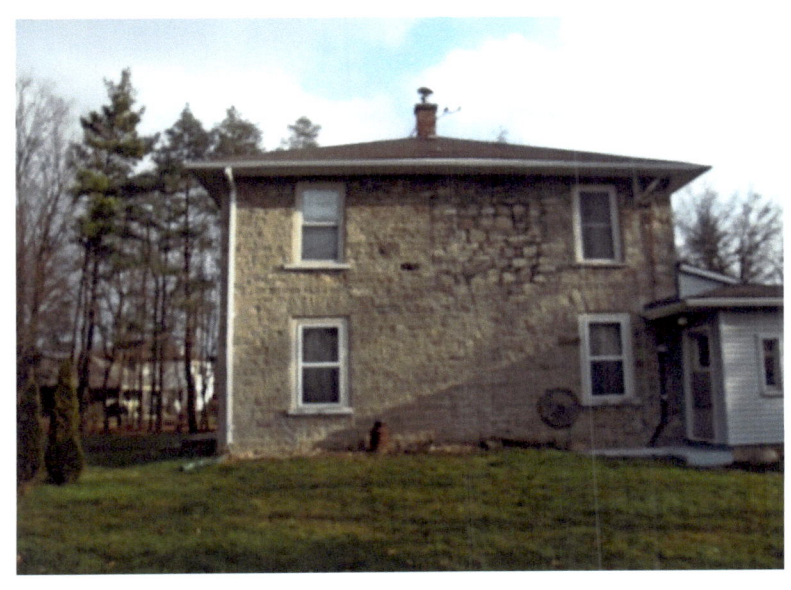

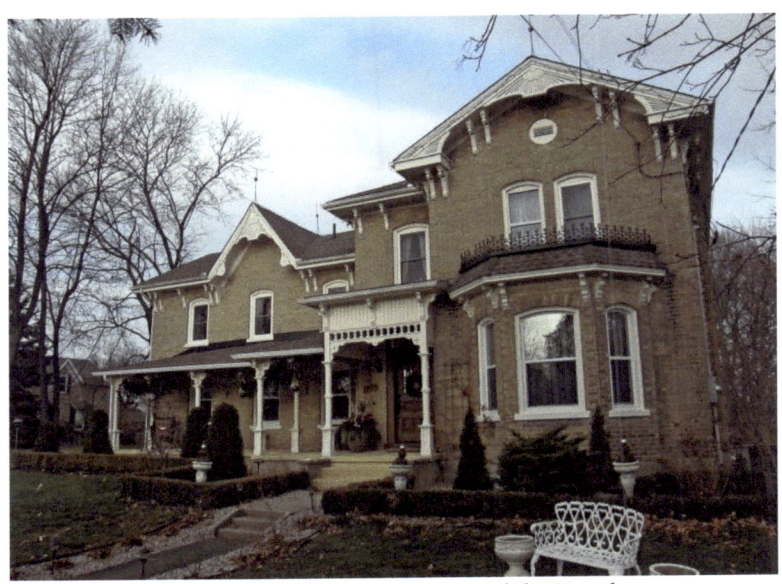

1266 Old Highway 8 - Old King's

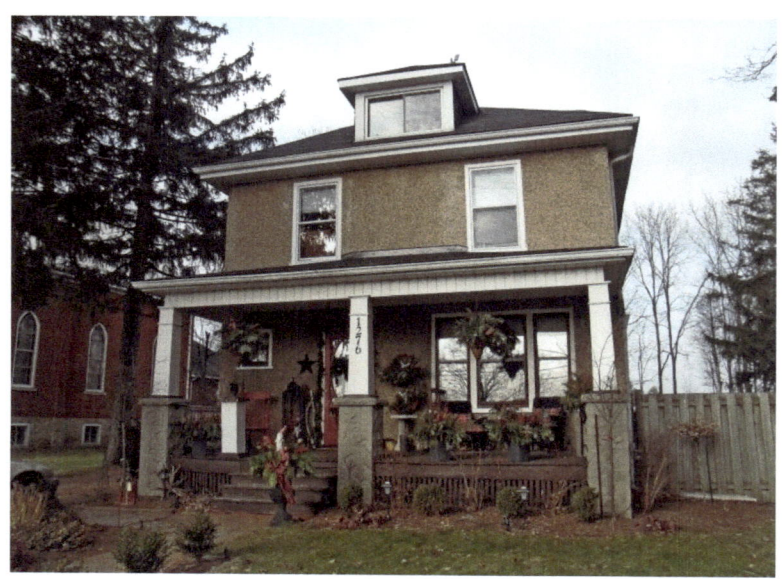

1276 Old Highway 8

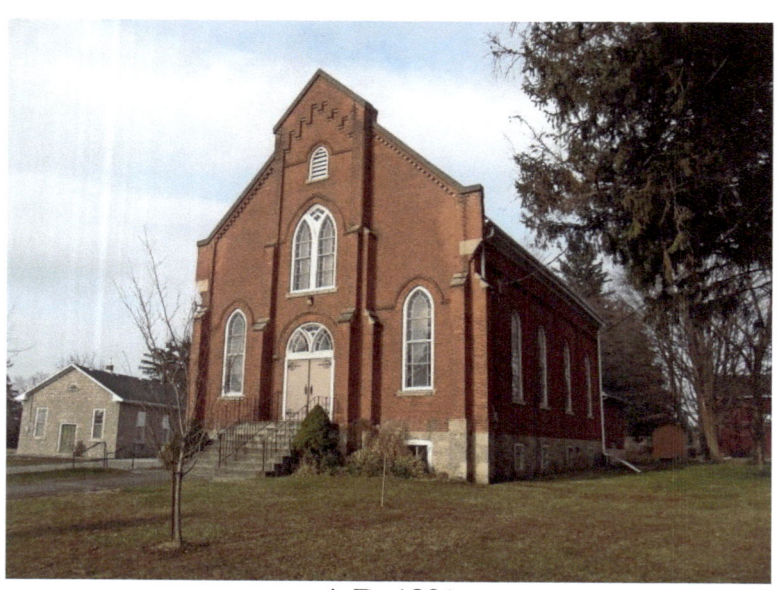

A.D. 1891

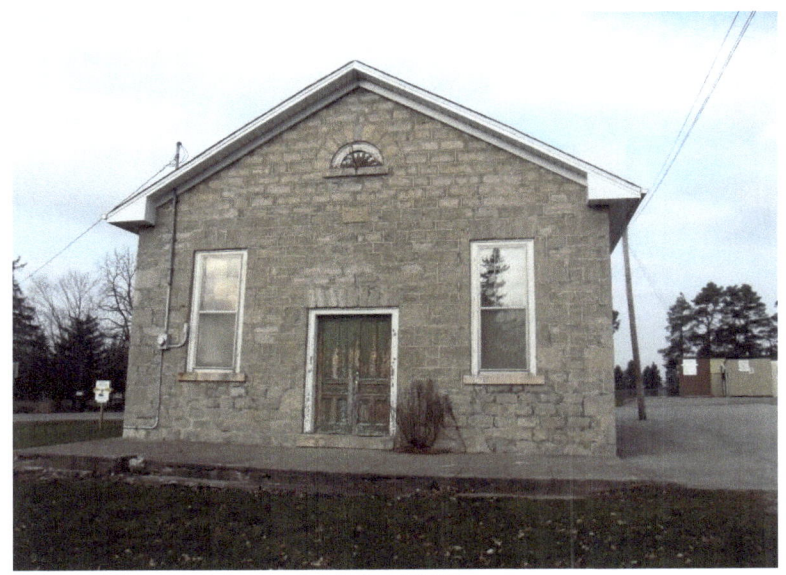

A.D. 1862

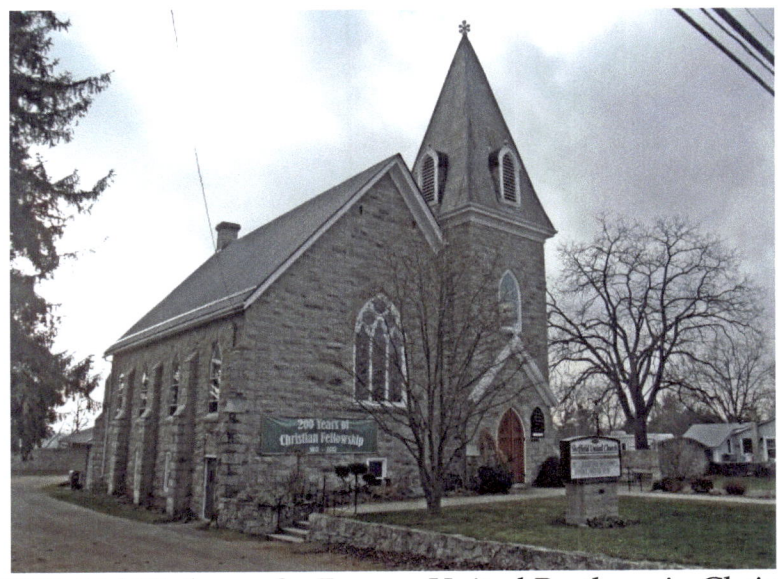

1283 Old Highway 8 - Former United Brethren in Christ
Church – 1894 - Sheffield United Church
200 Years of Christian Fellowship 1812-2012

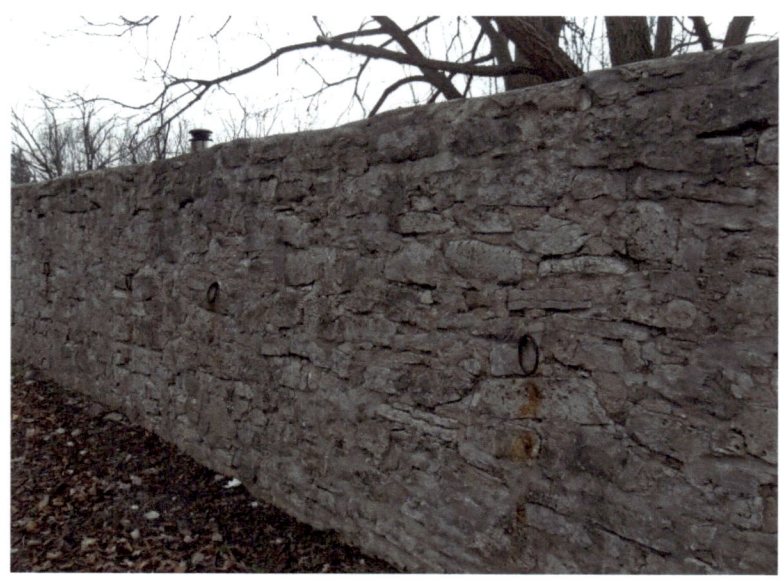

Rings in the wall for tying up the horses - Sheffield United Church

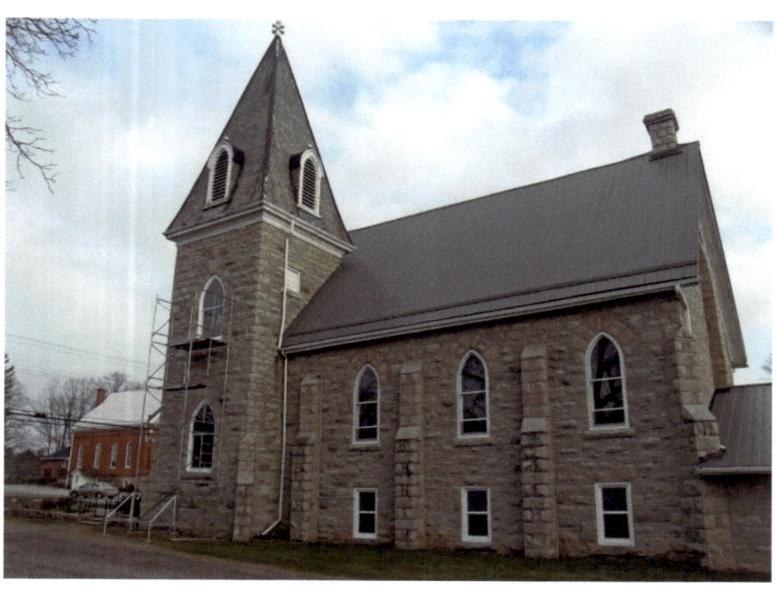

Kirkwall

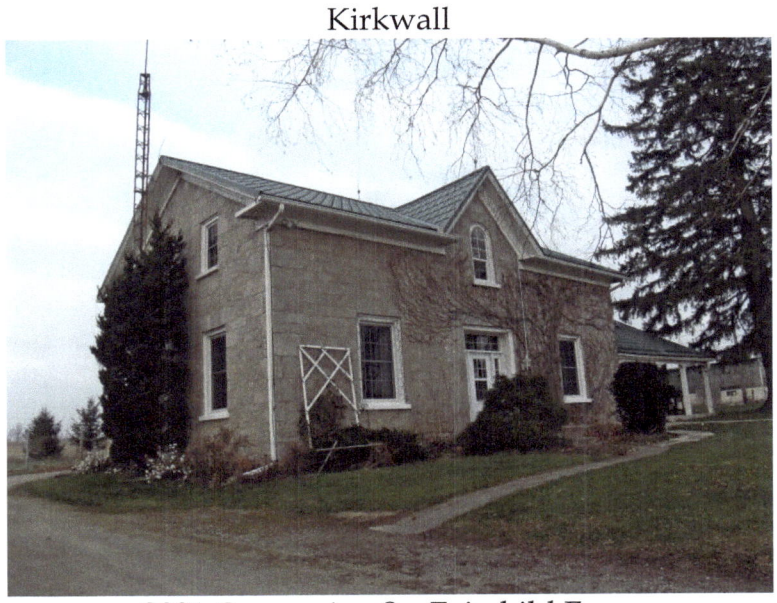

2091 Concession 8 – Fairchild Farm

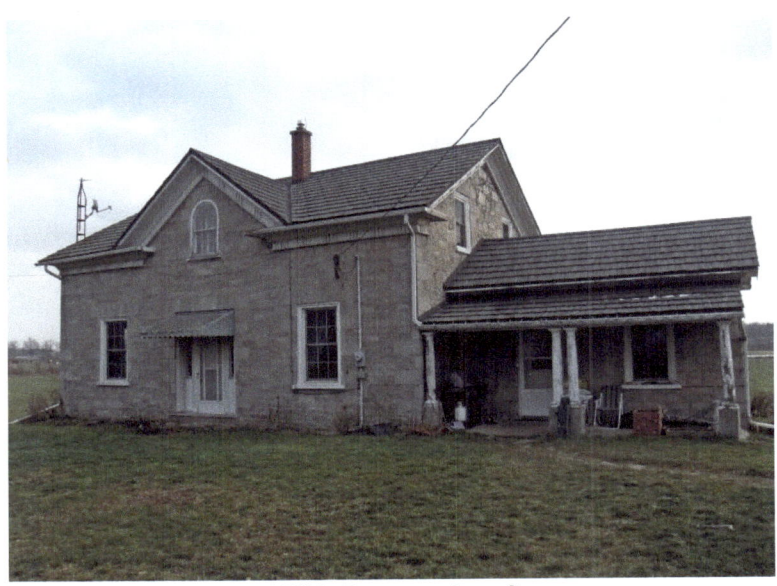

1926 Concession 8

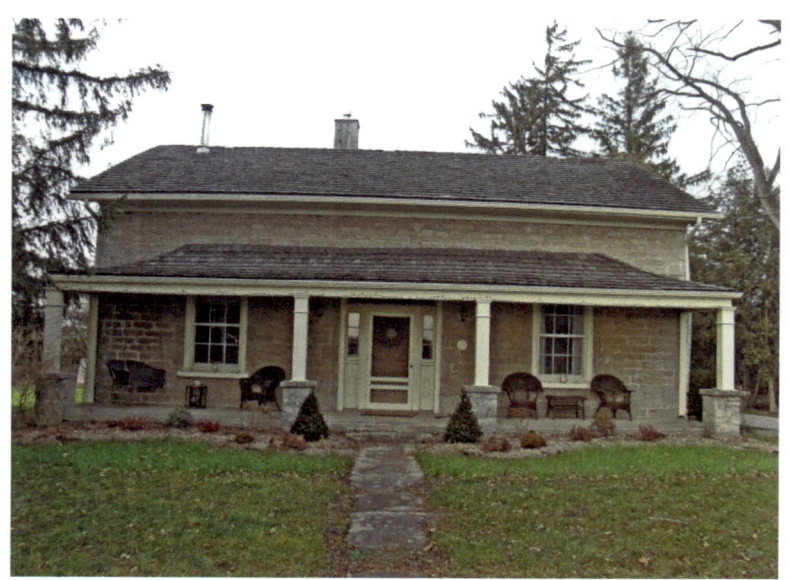

1905 Concession 8

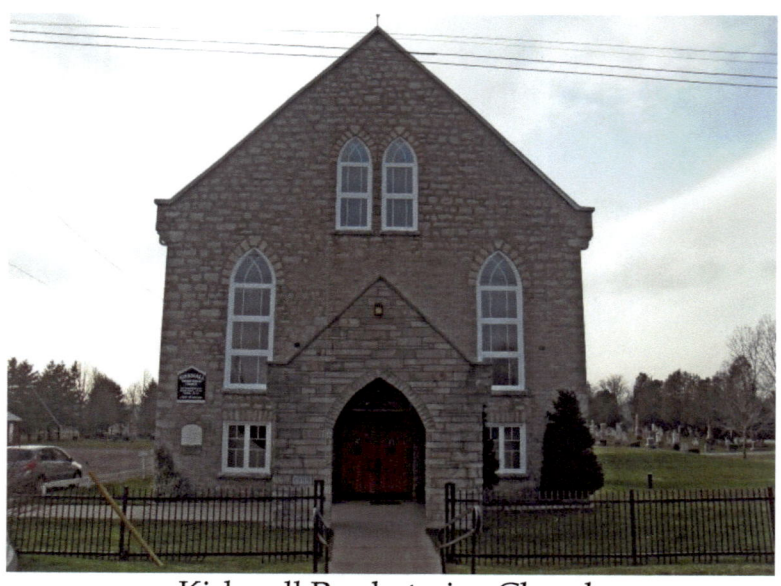

Kirkwall Presbyterian Church
1886 Concession 8 West and Kirkwall Road
Built 1848, Remodelled 1900

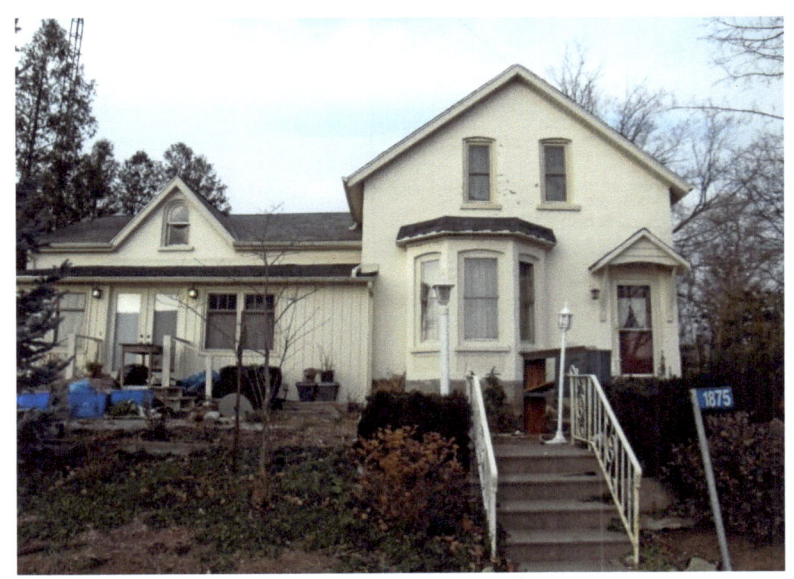

1875 Concession 8

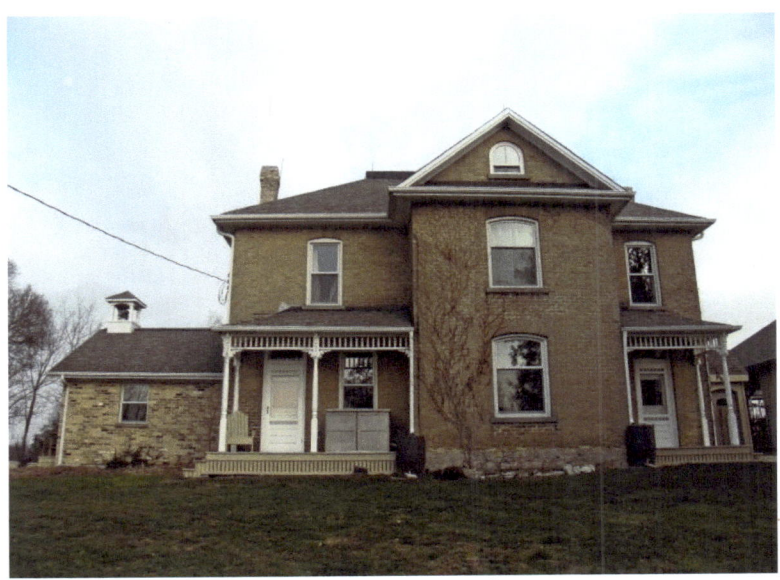

Kirkwall Road

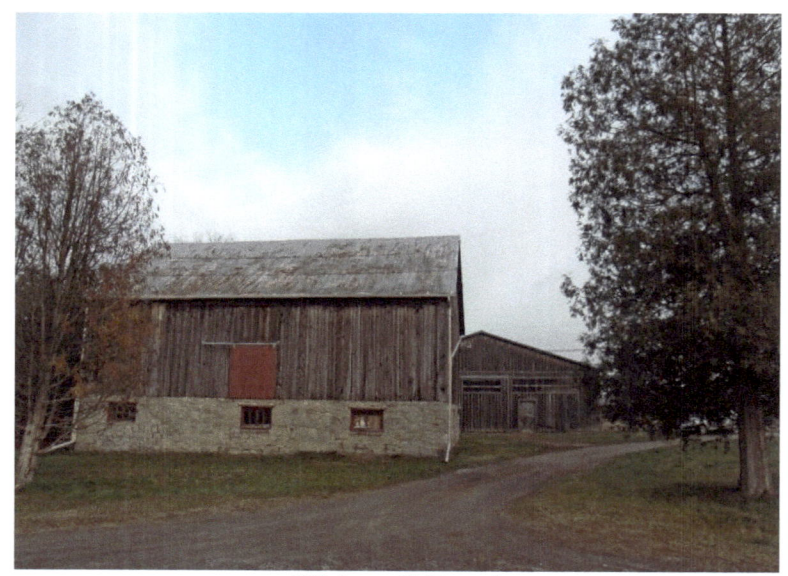

Kirkwall Road

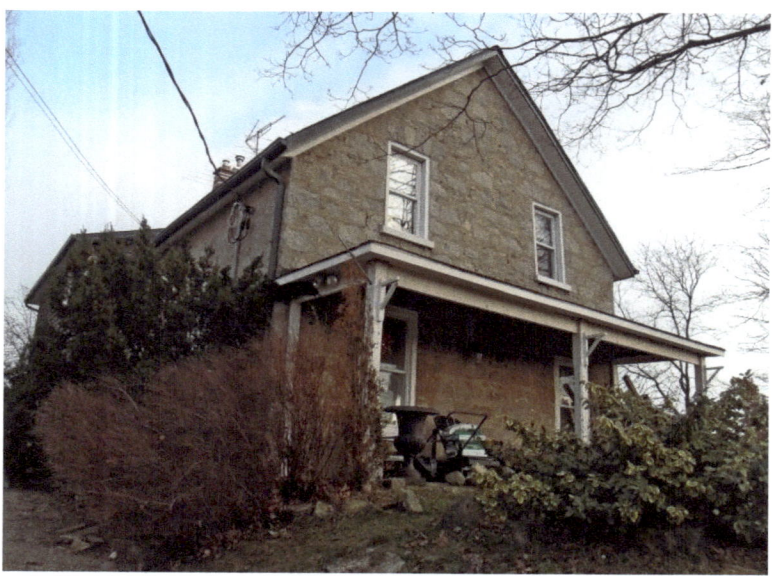

Kirkwall Road

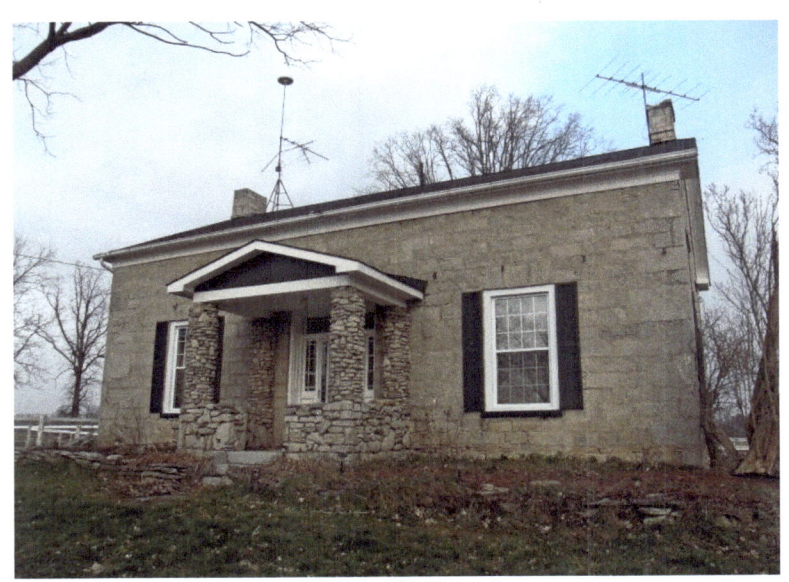

Kirkwall Road

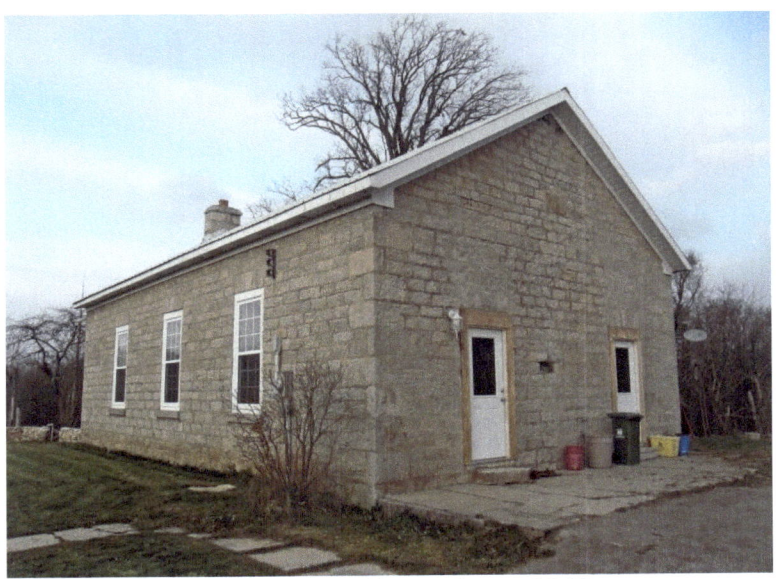

1434 Kirkwall Road – c. 1862

Westfield Heritage Village

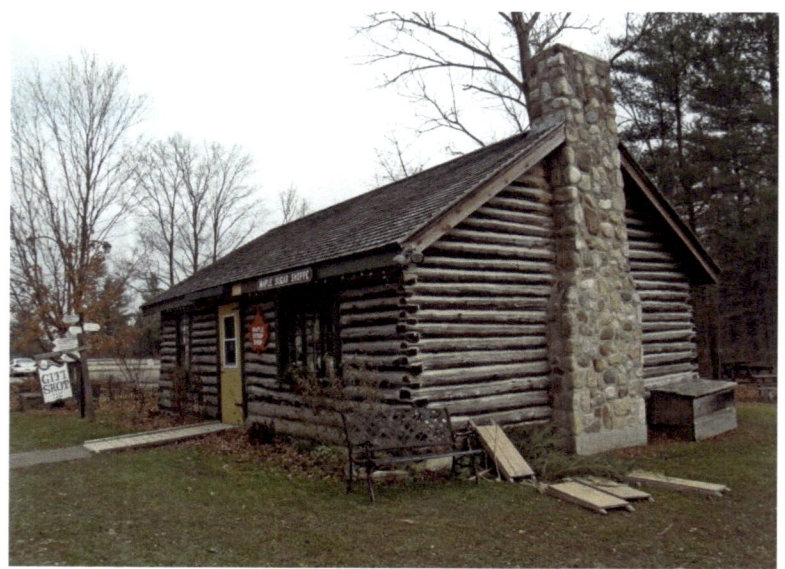

RCMP - 1934

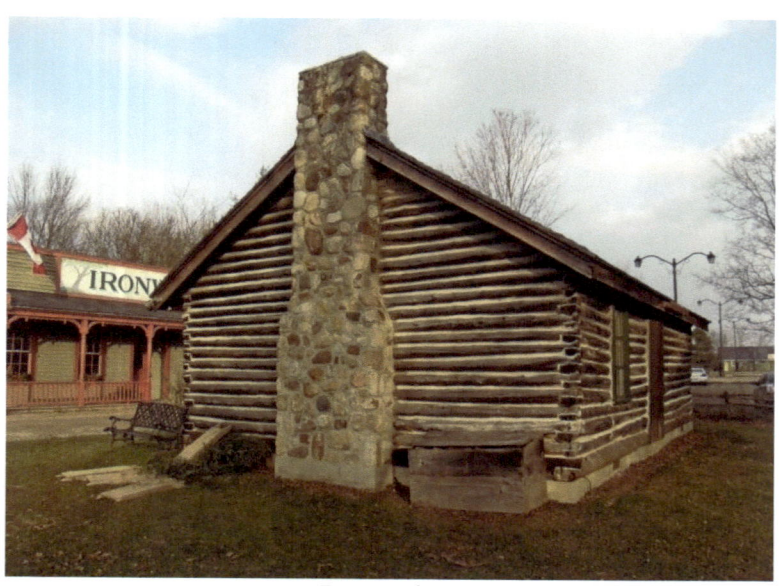

Log cabin

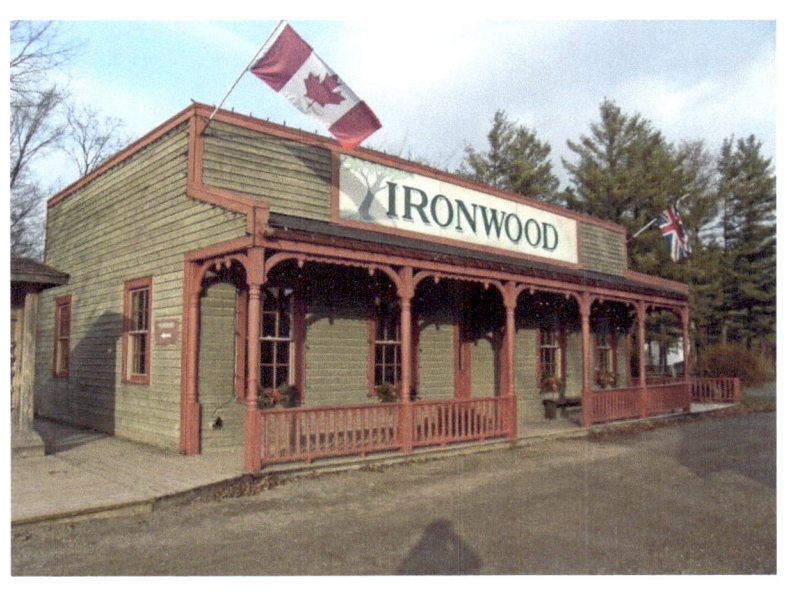

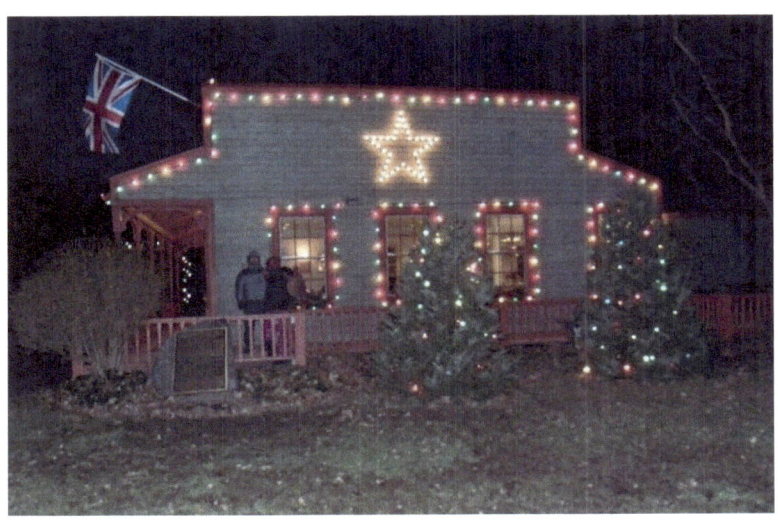

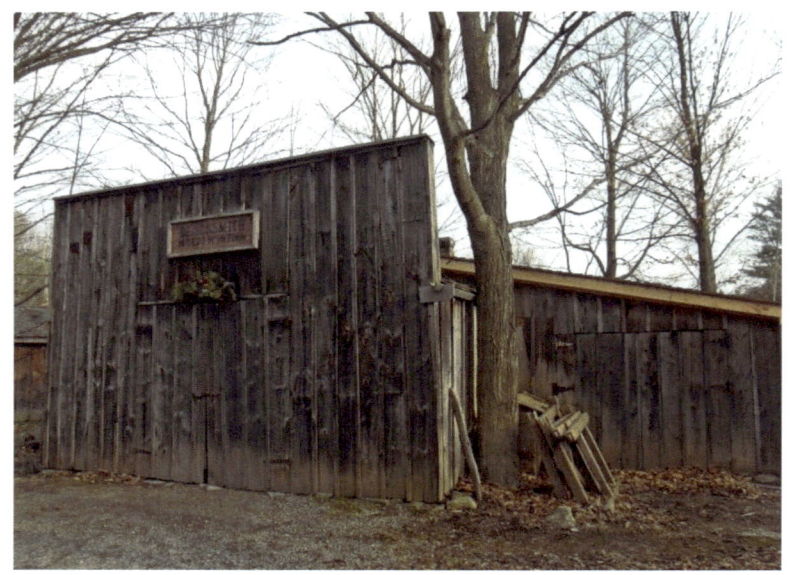

Blacksmith shop

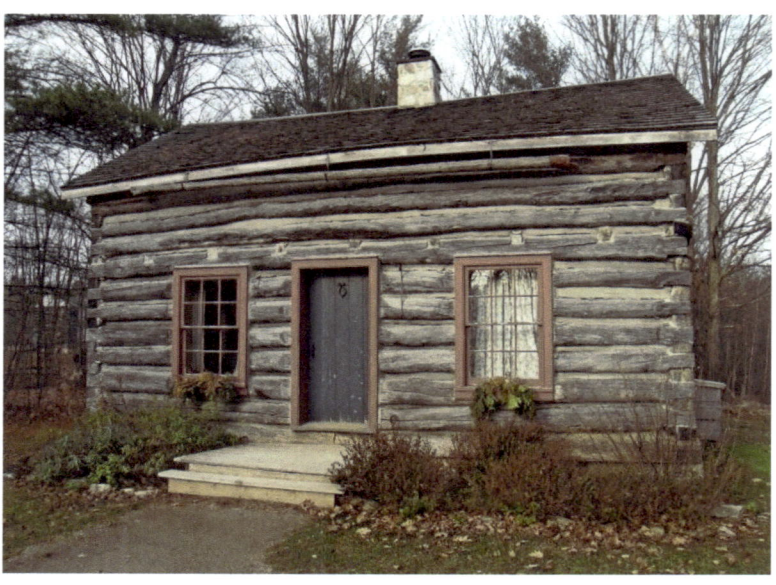

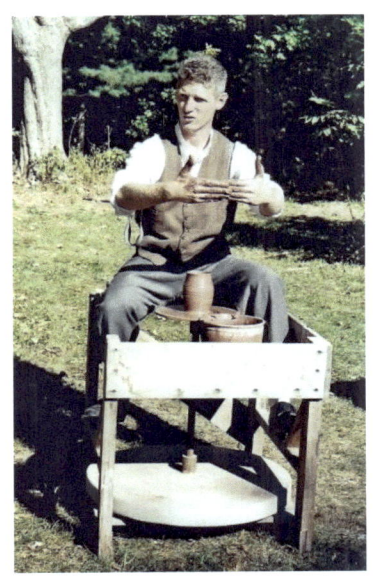

Pottery Making

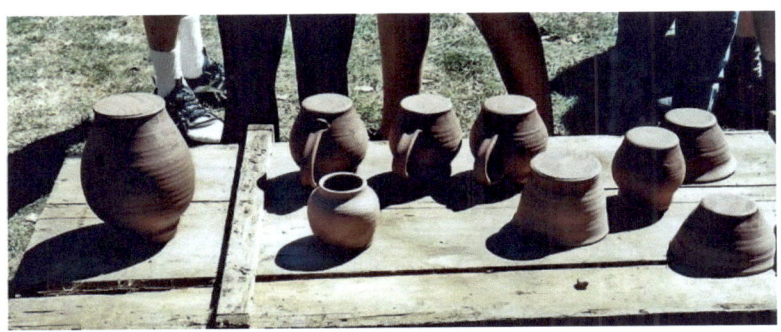

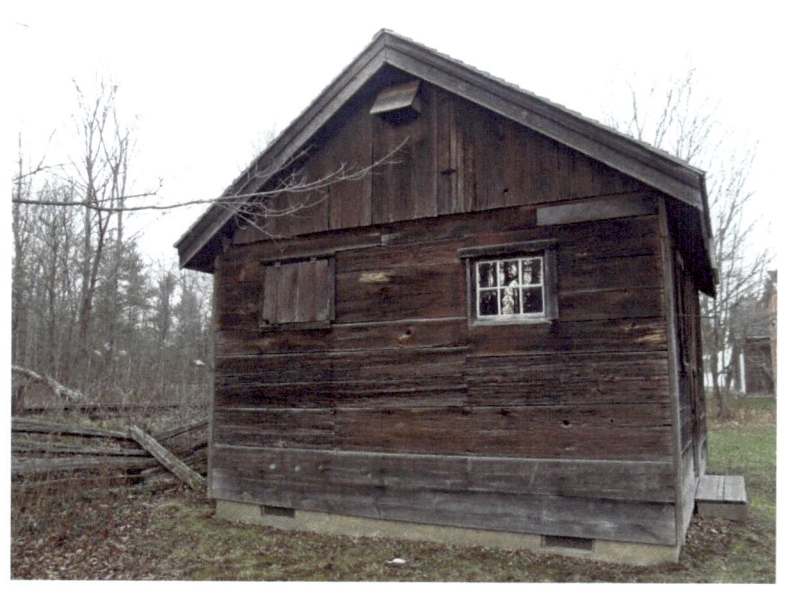

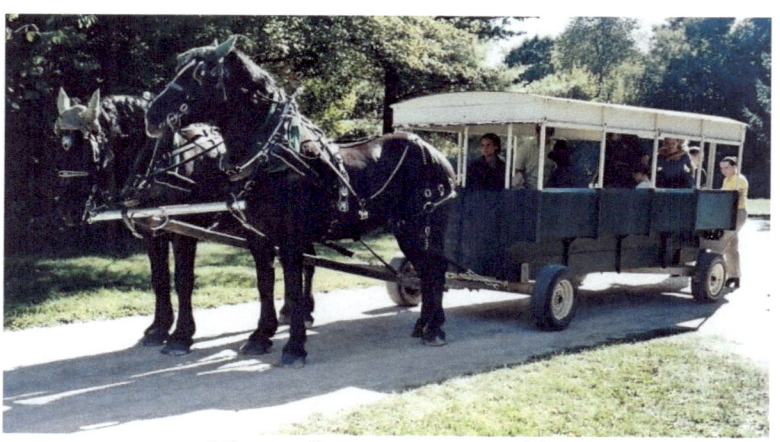

Horse-drawn wagon ride

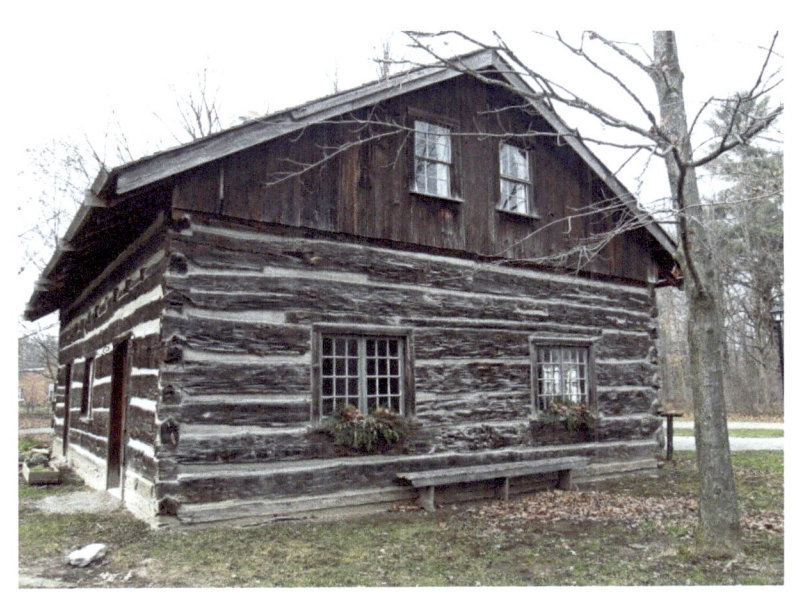

Daubigny's Inn c. 1820

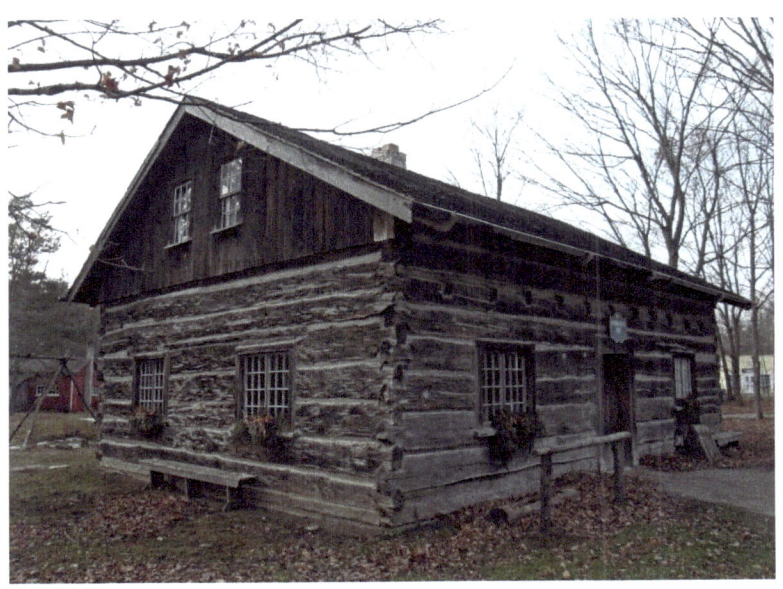

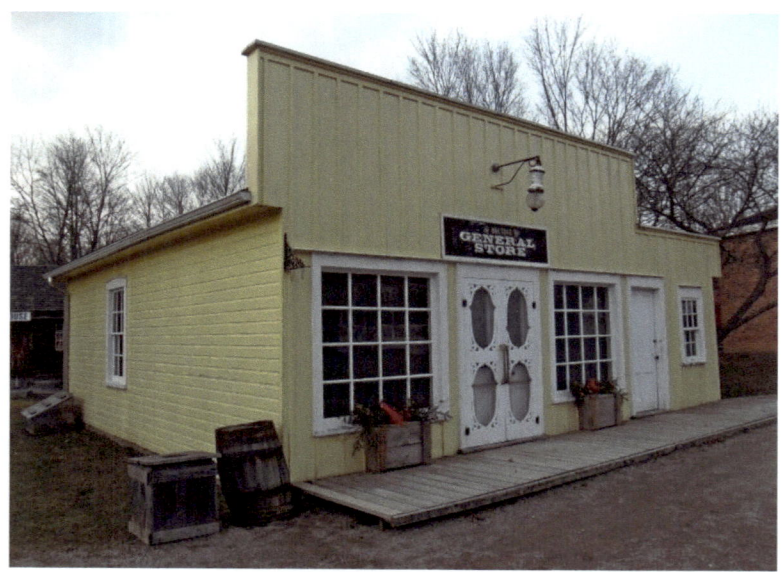

General Store established 1848

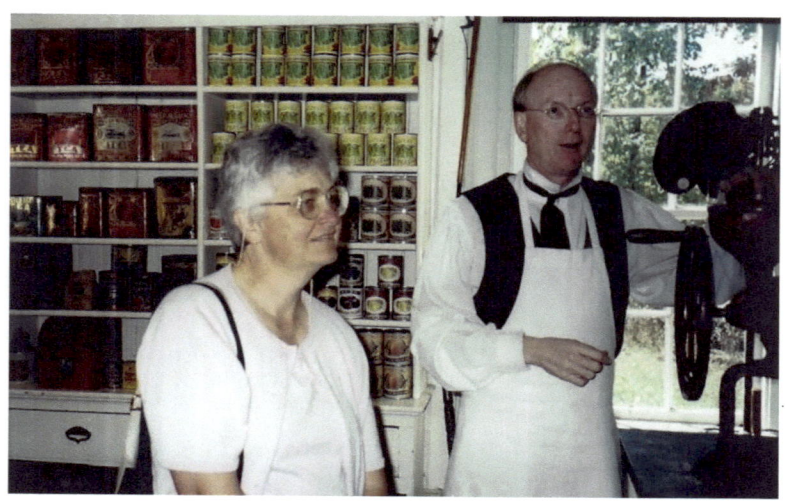

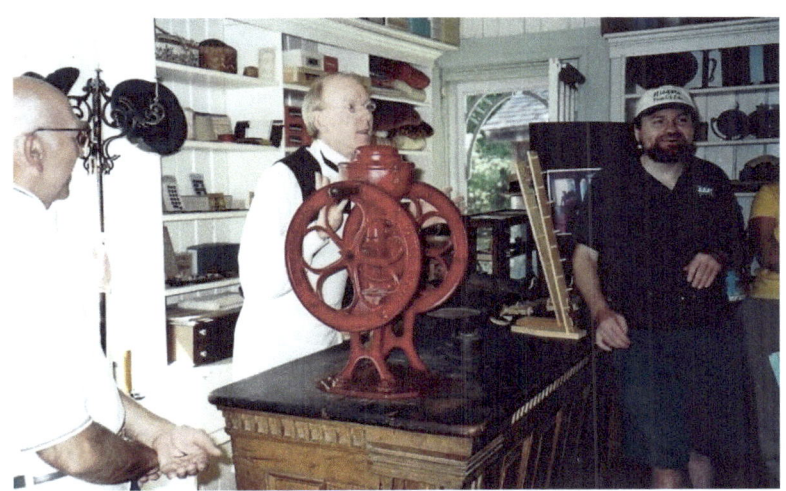

Coffee Grinder

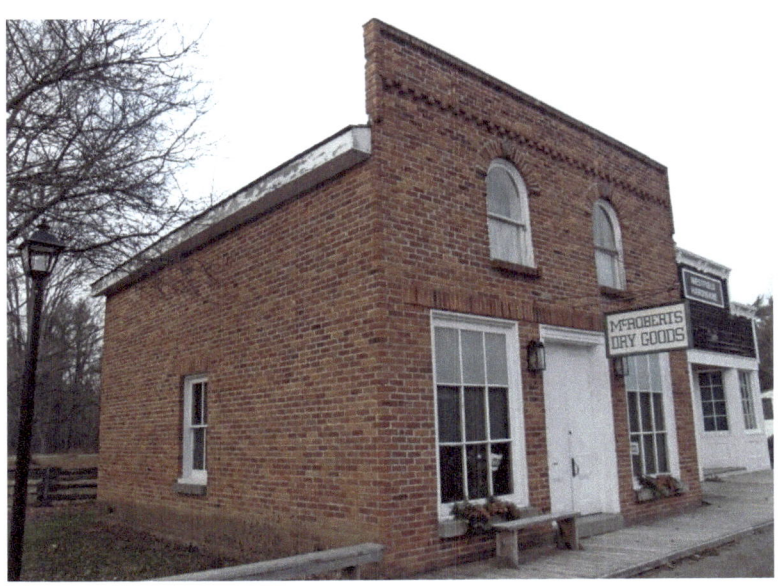

Dry Goods Store

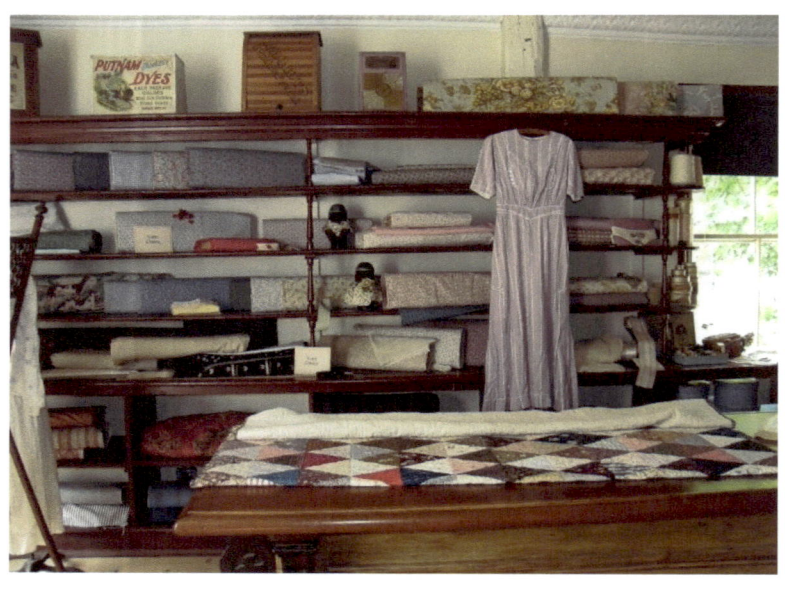

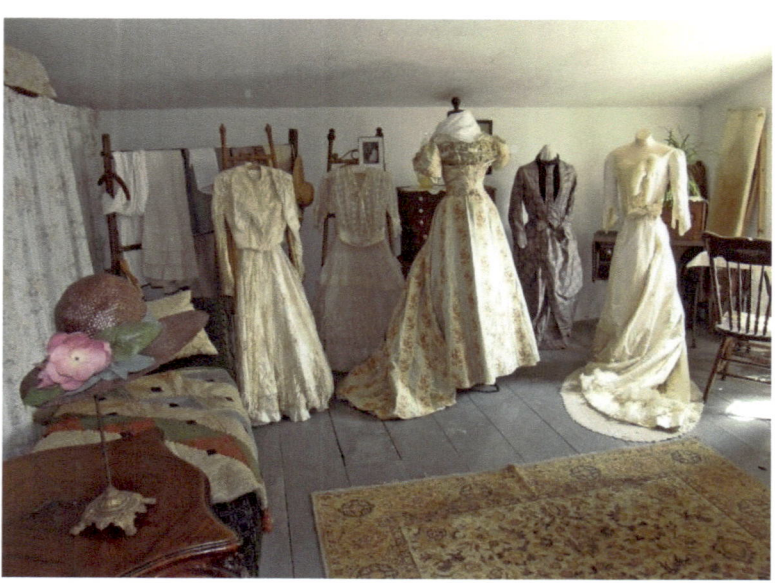

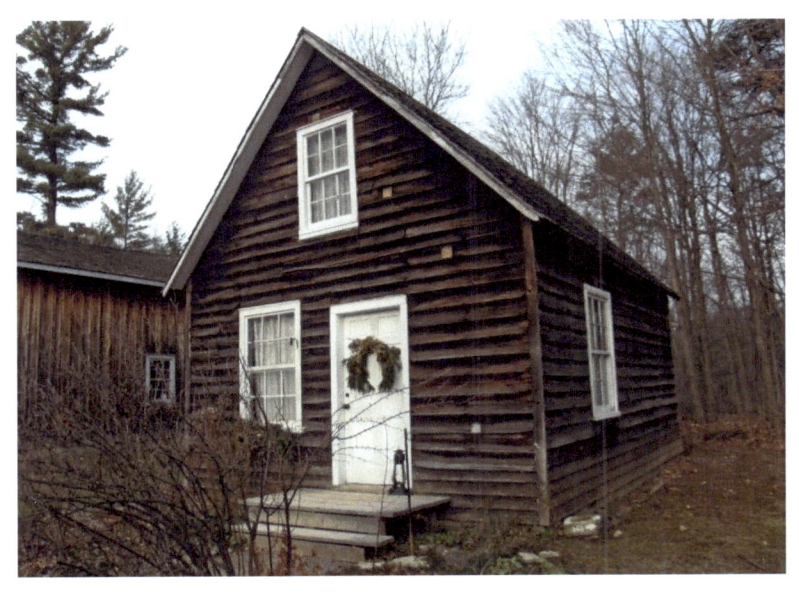

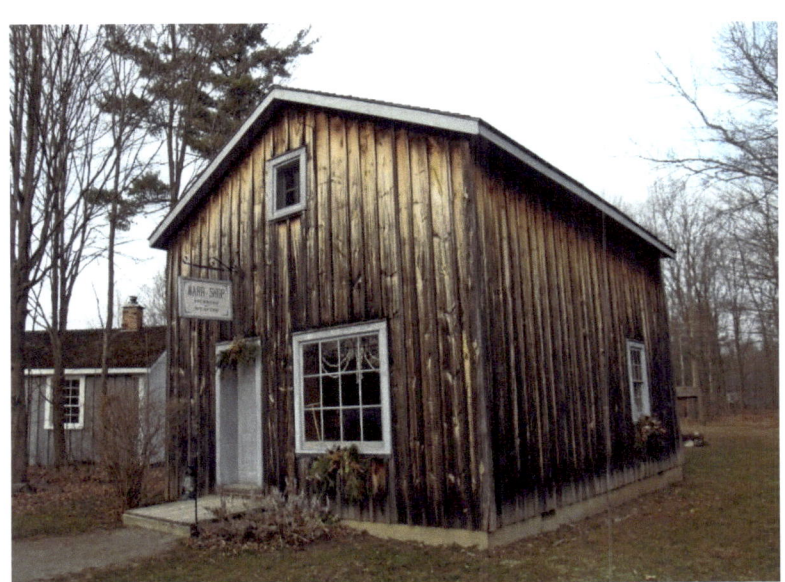

Spinning and Weaving Shop

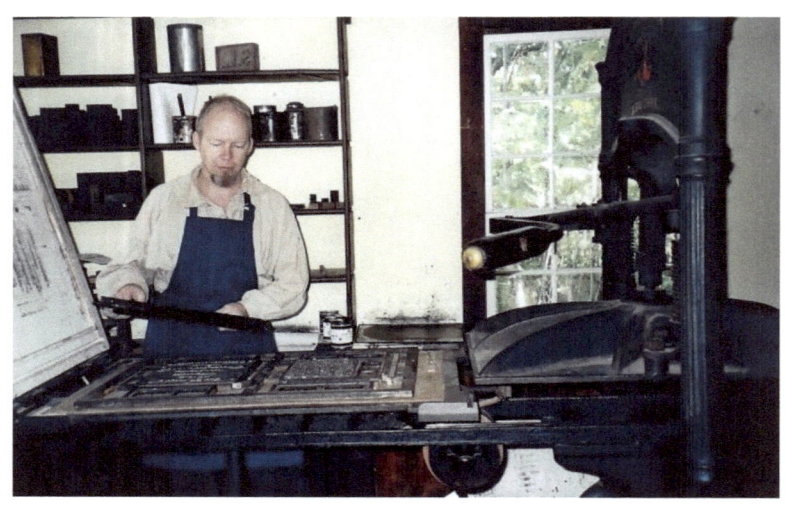

In the Print Shop

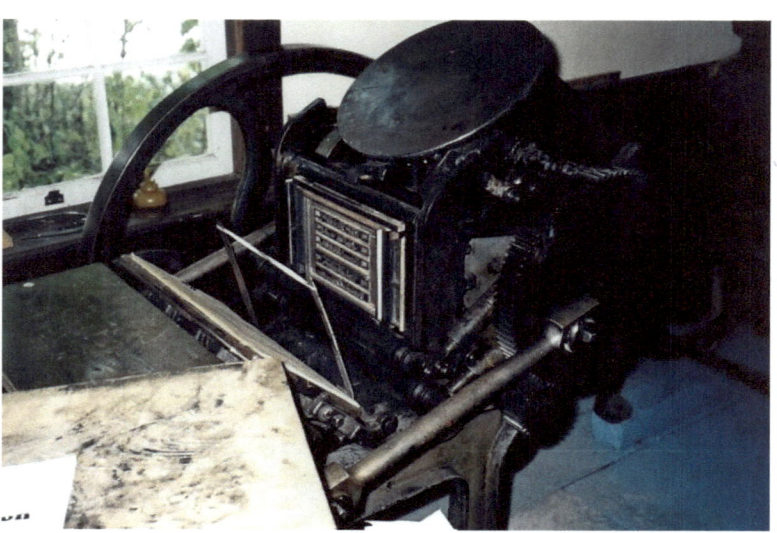

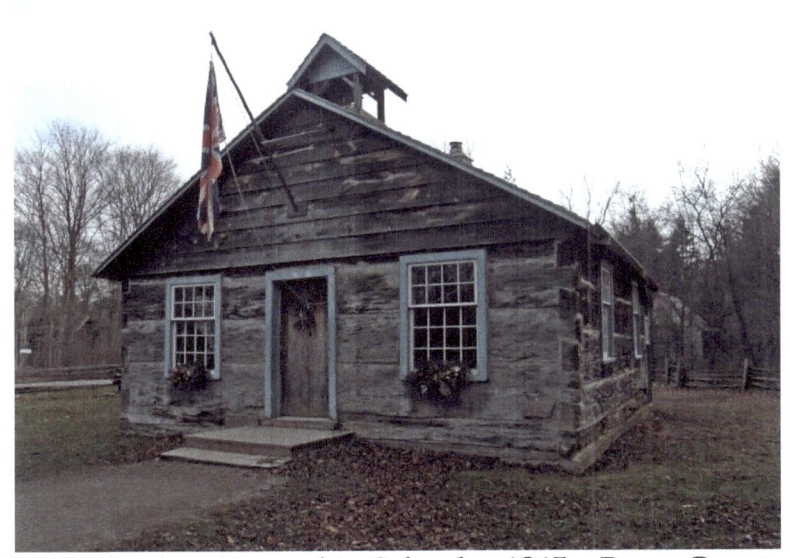

S.S. 24 Burford Township School c. 1845 – Brant County

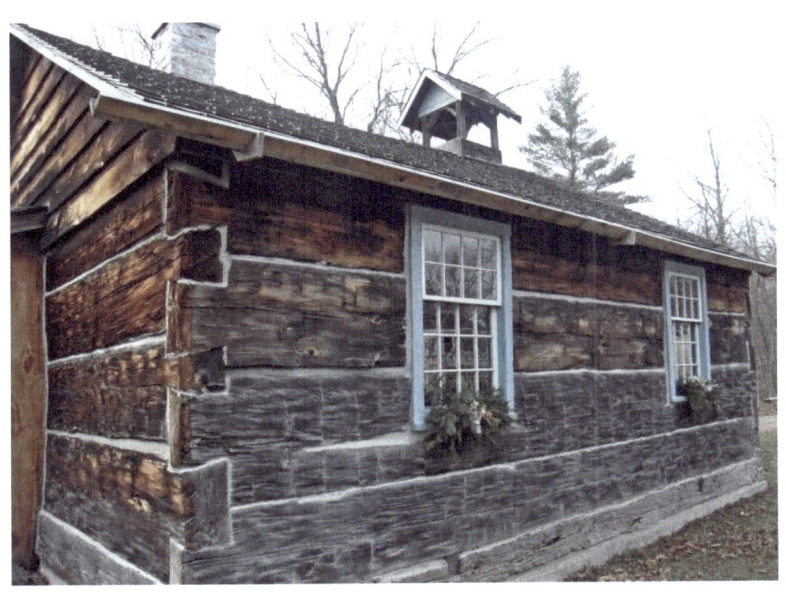

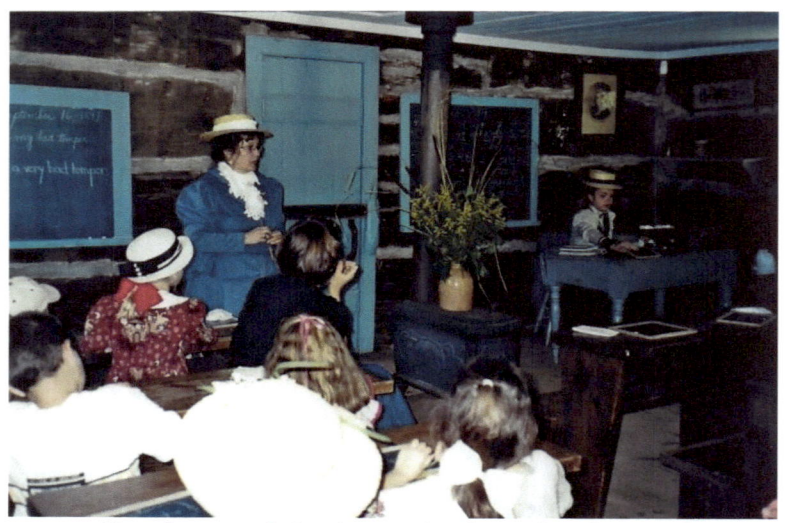
Teacher and Assistant in the school room

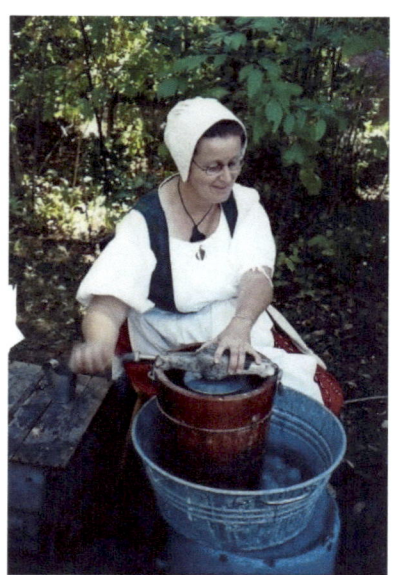
Making Ice Cream

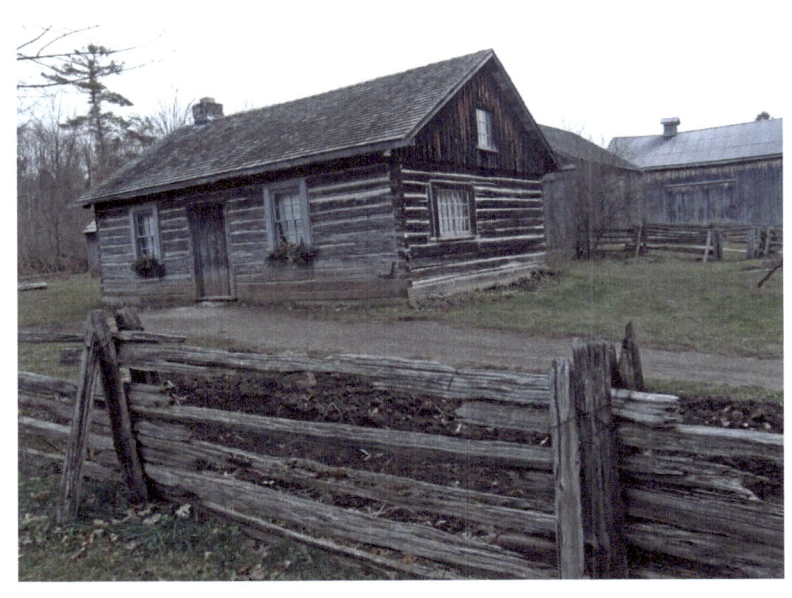

Lockhart House – 1845 – Oxford County

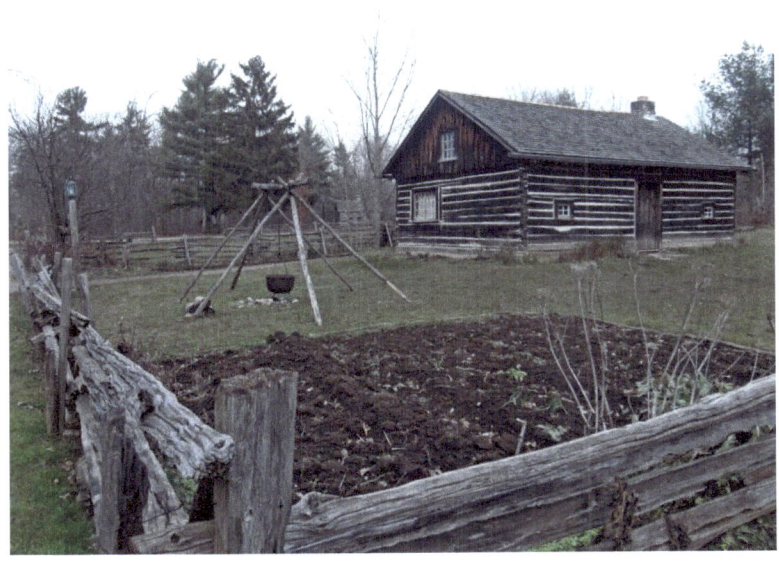

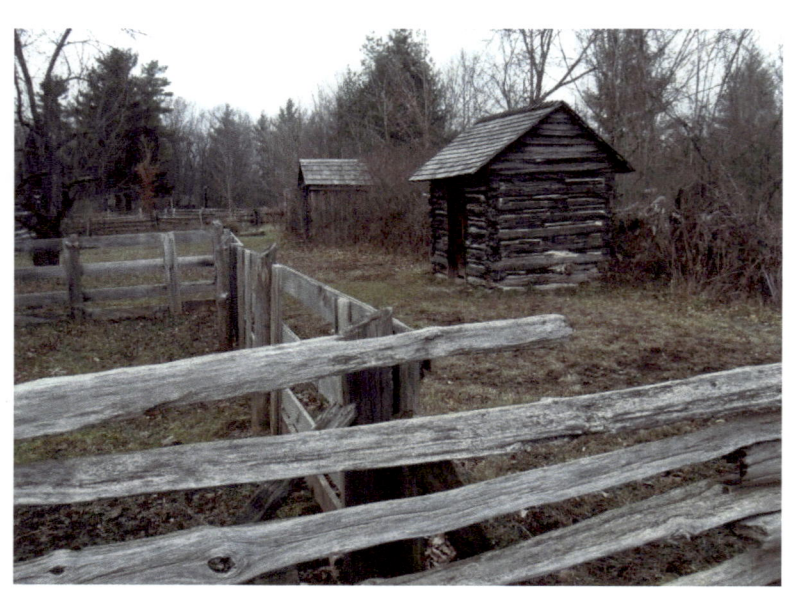

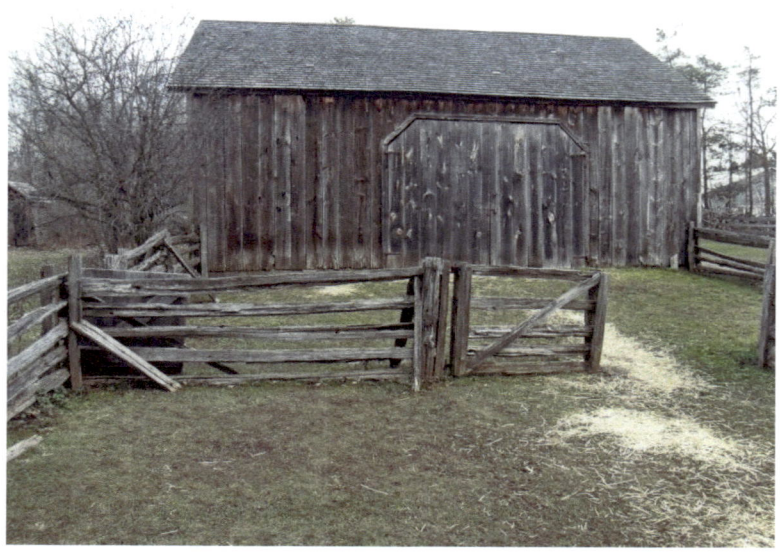

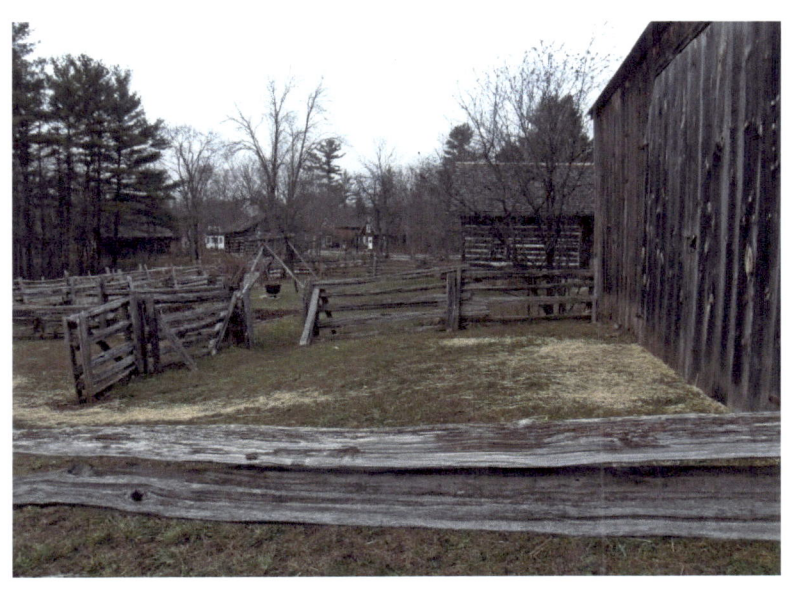

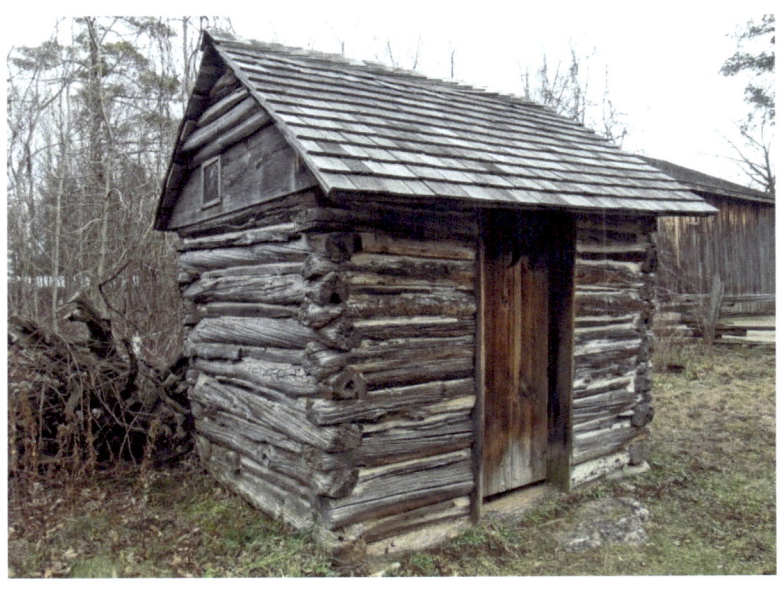

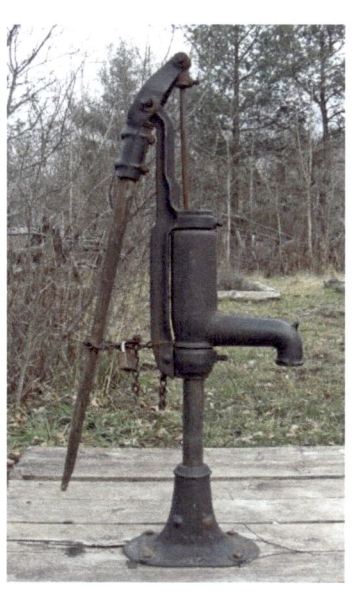

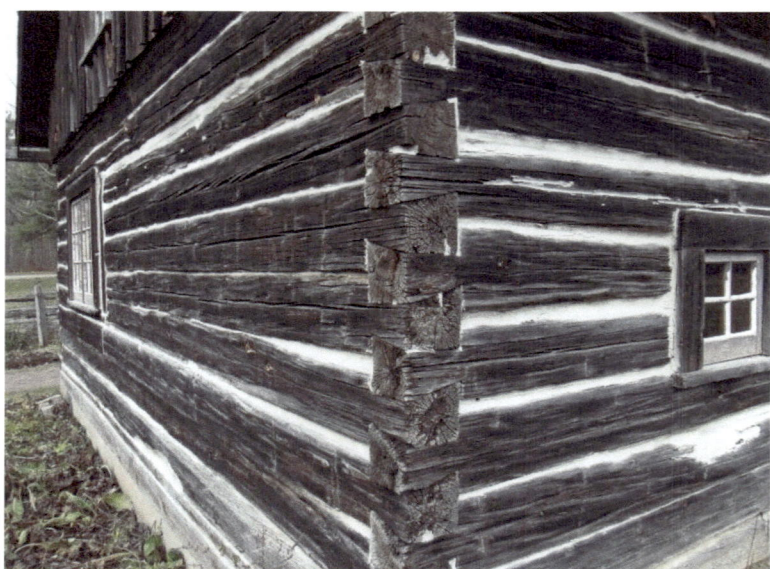

Corner showing construction of the log cabin

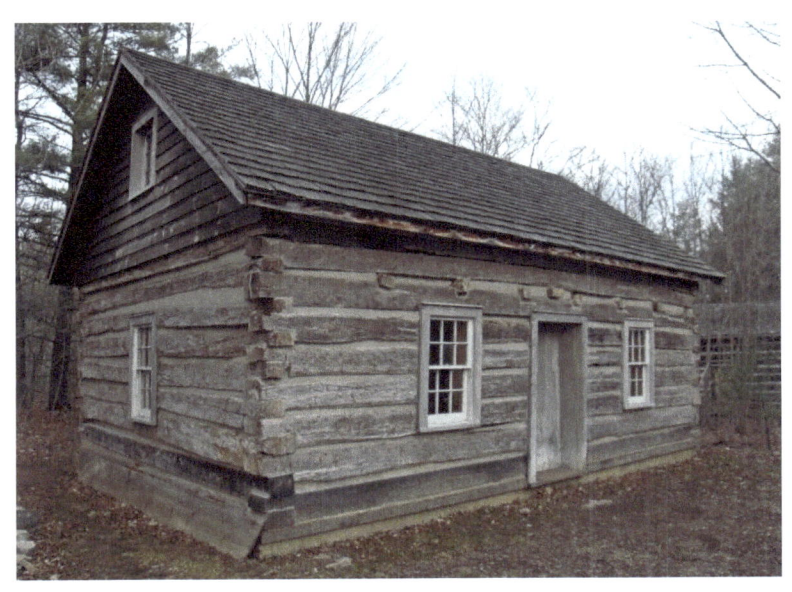

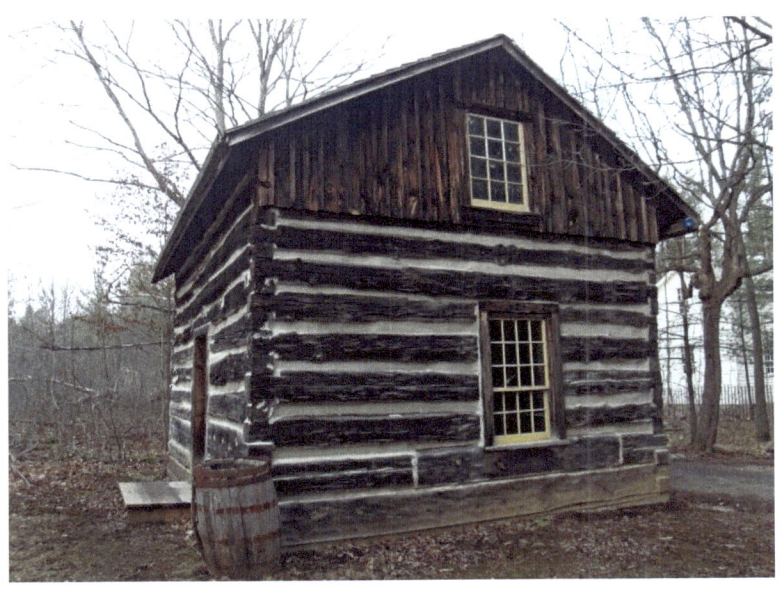

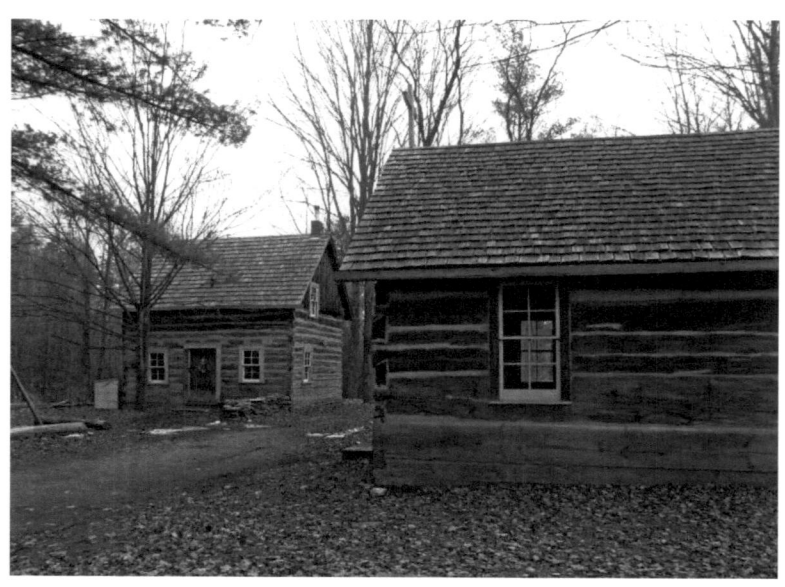

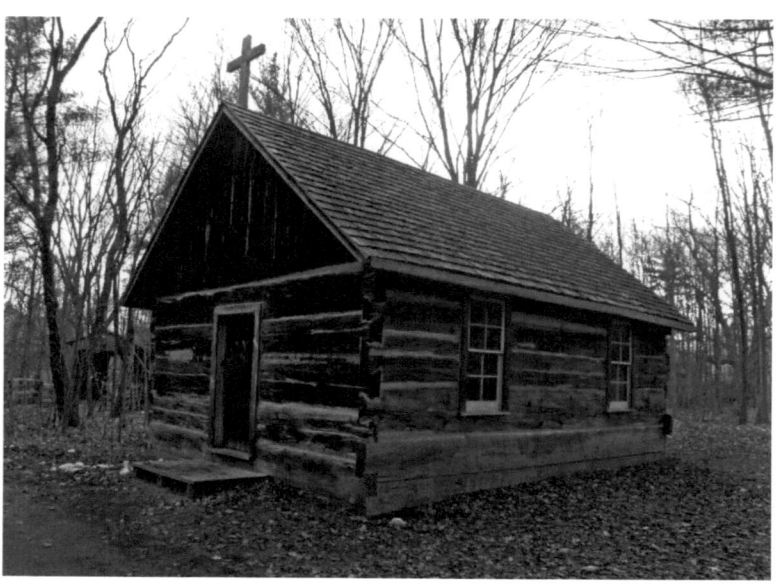

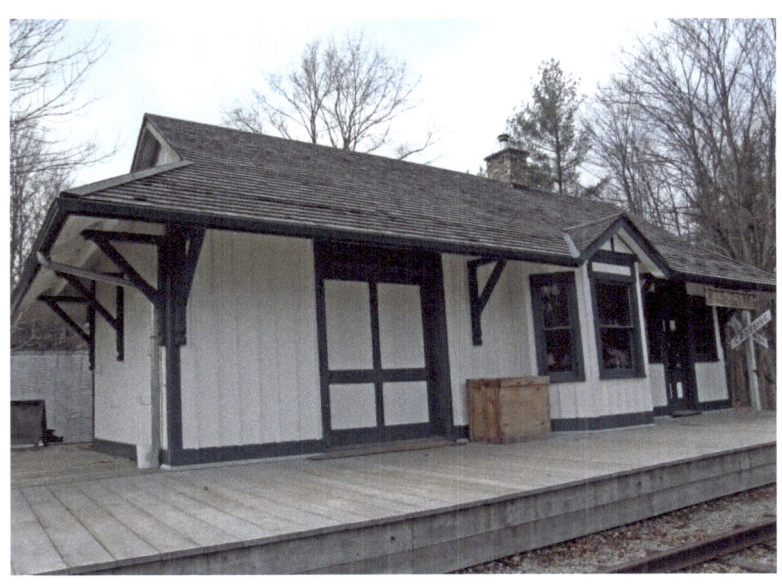

The Jerseyville Railway Station was built in 1896 when ten trains a day ran between Hamilton and Brantford.

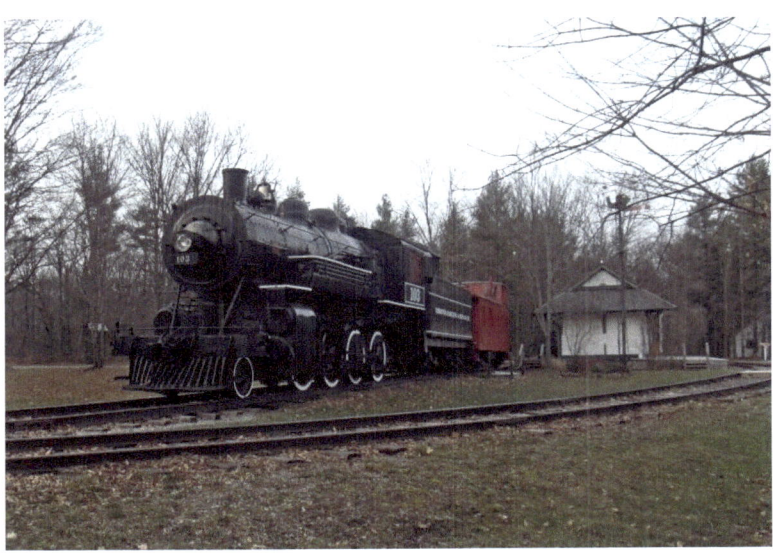

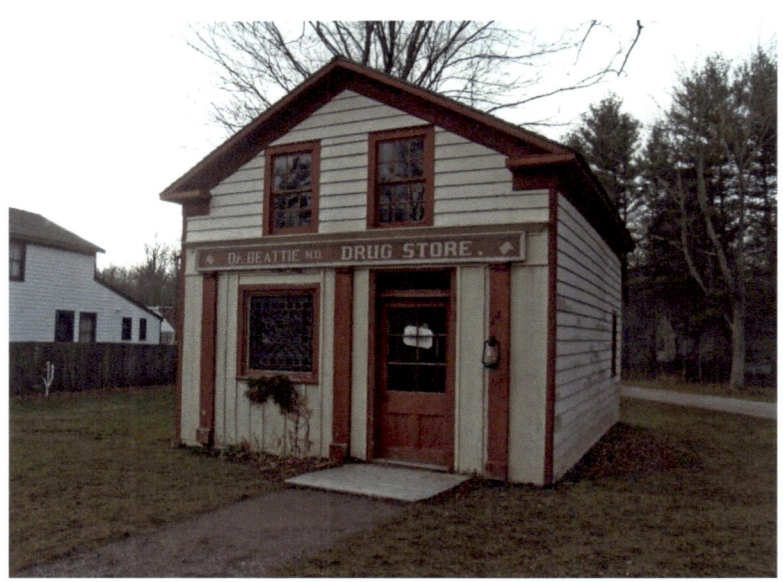

Drug Store - Clapboard building

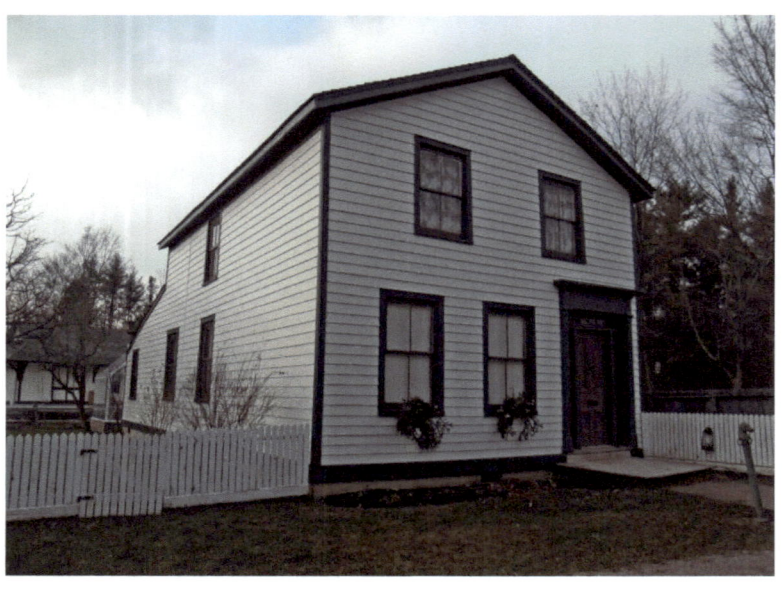

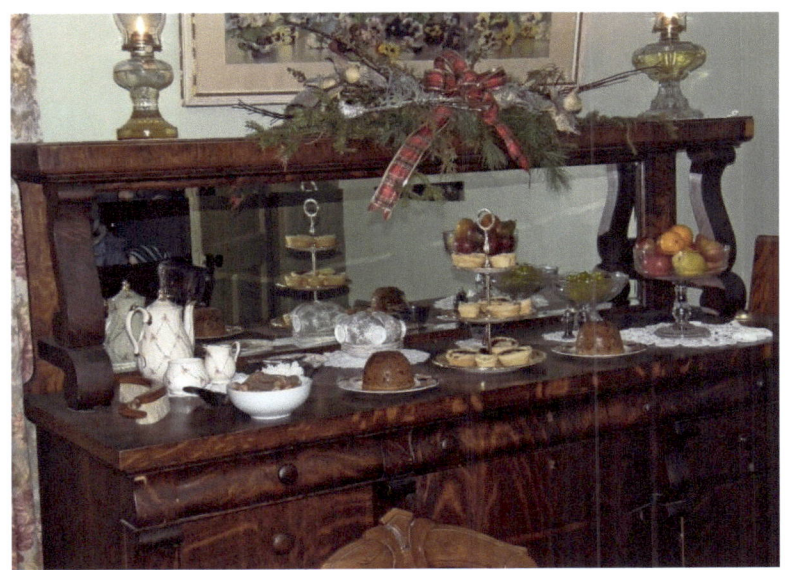
Sideboard with desserts ready

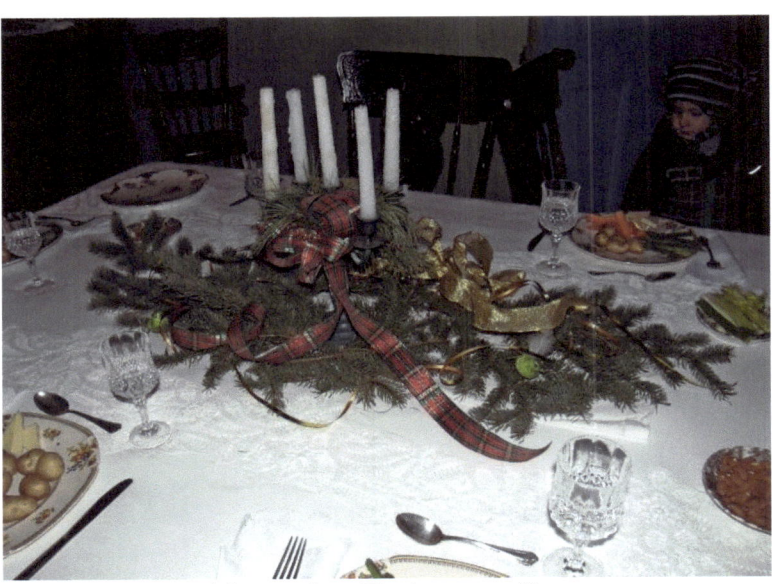
Table set for Christmas dinner

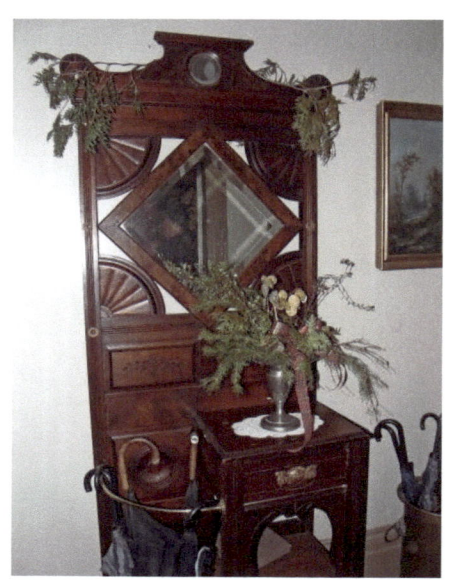

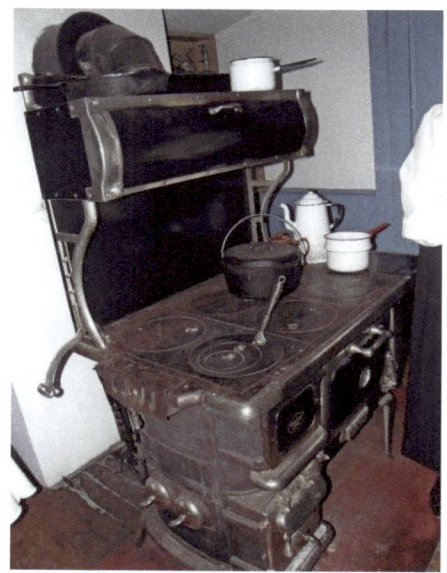

Wood stove

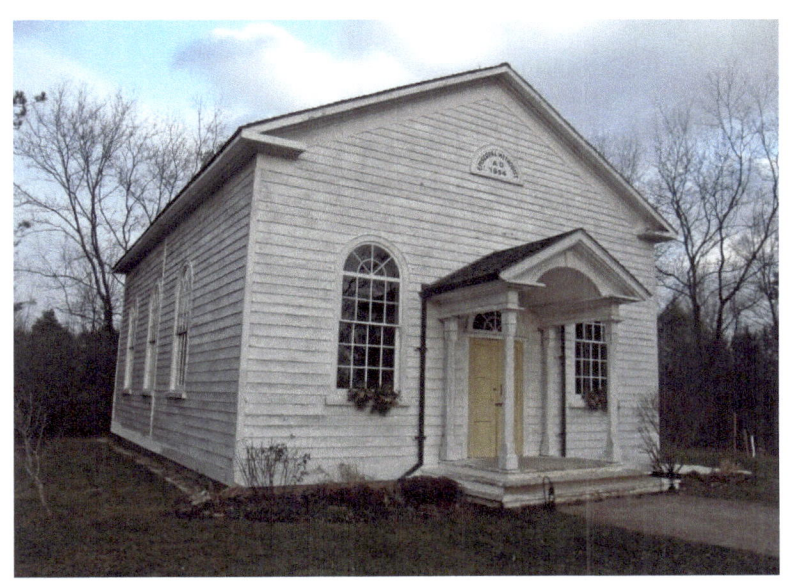

Episcopal Methodist Church A.D. 1854

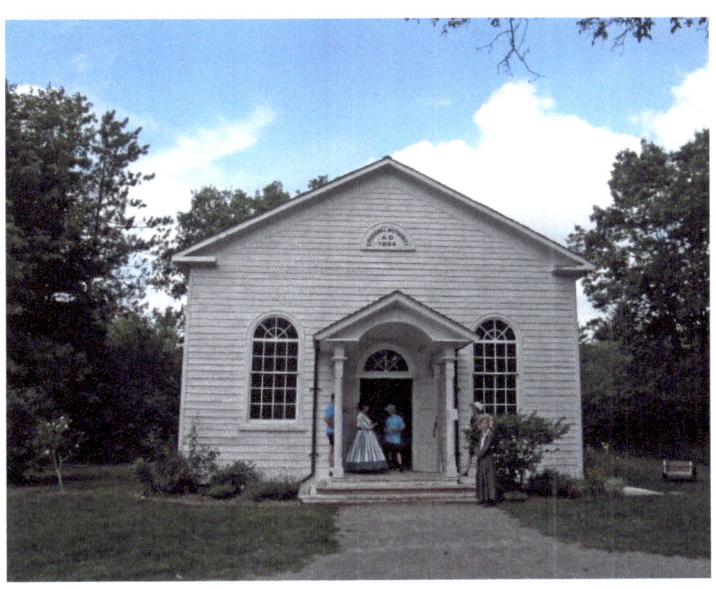

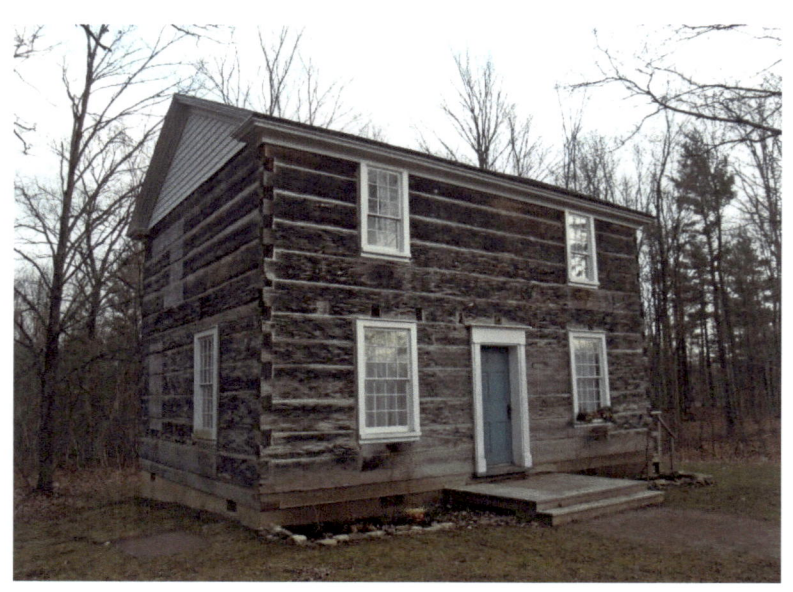

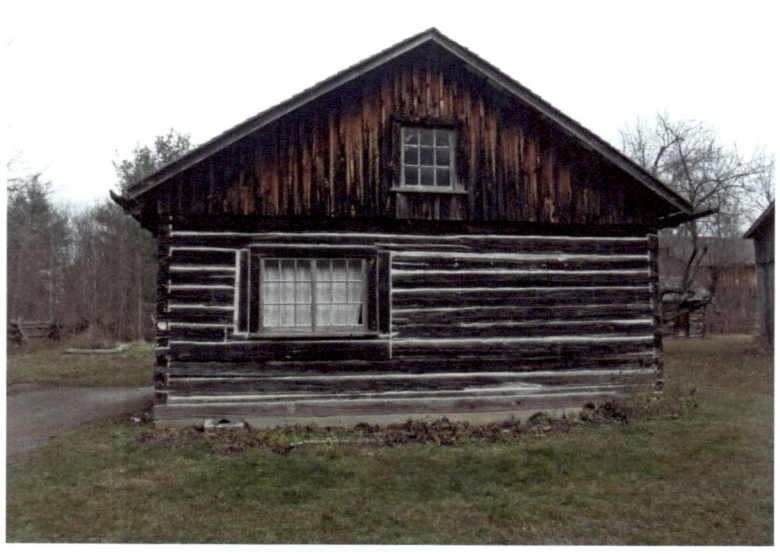

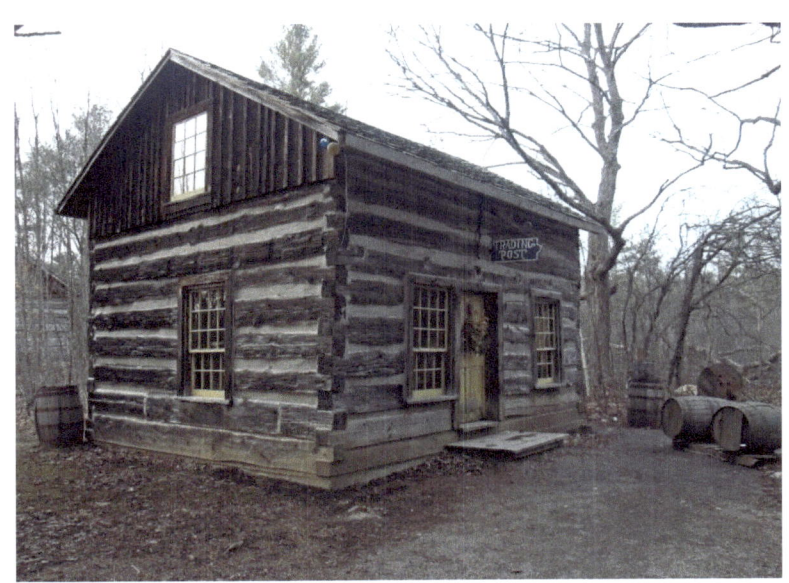

Trading Post

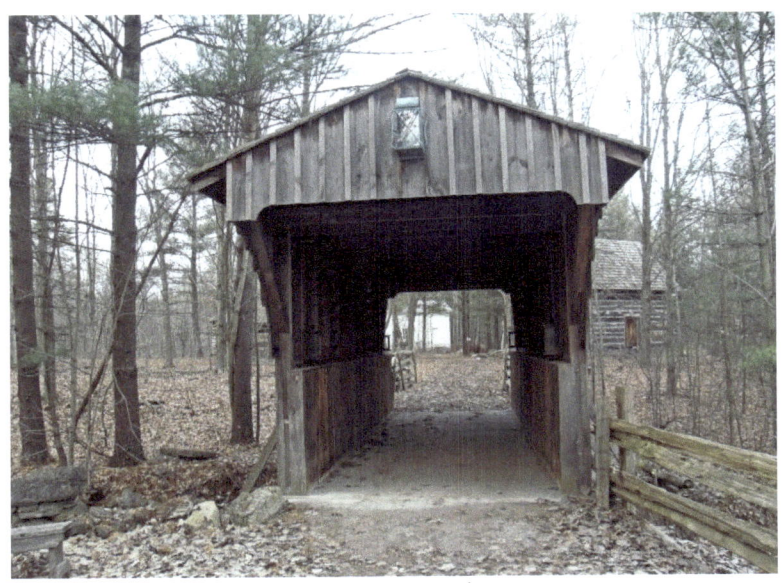

Covered Bridge

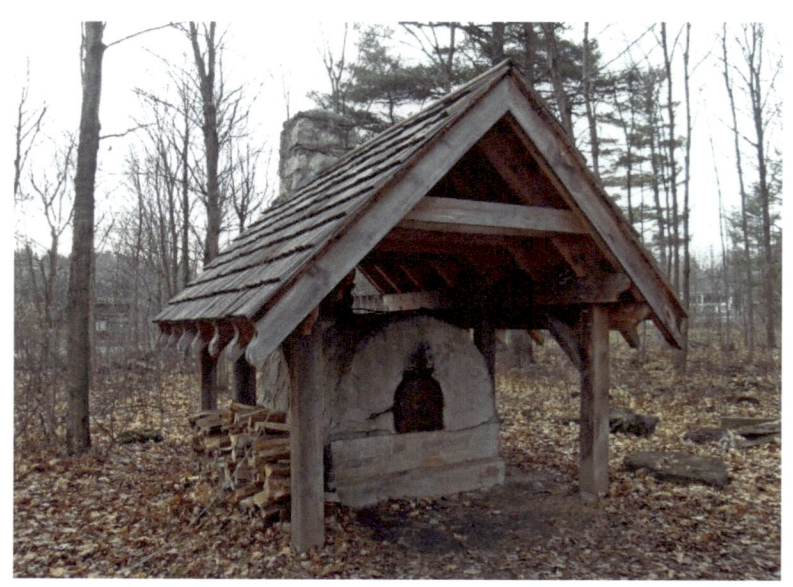
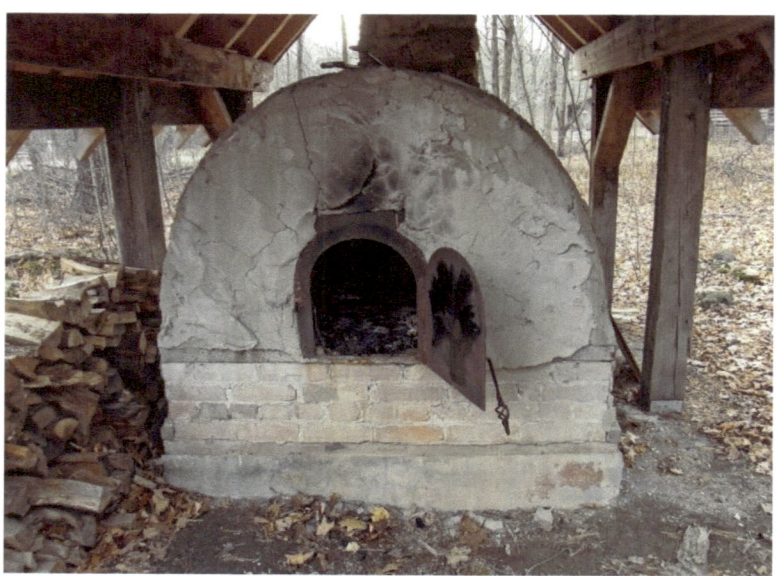

Outdoor oven

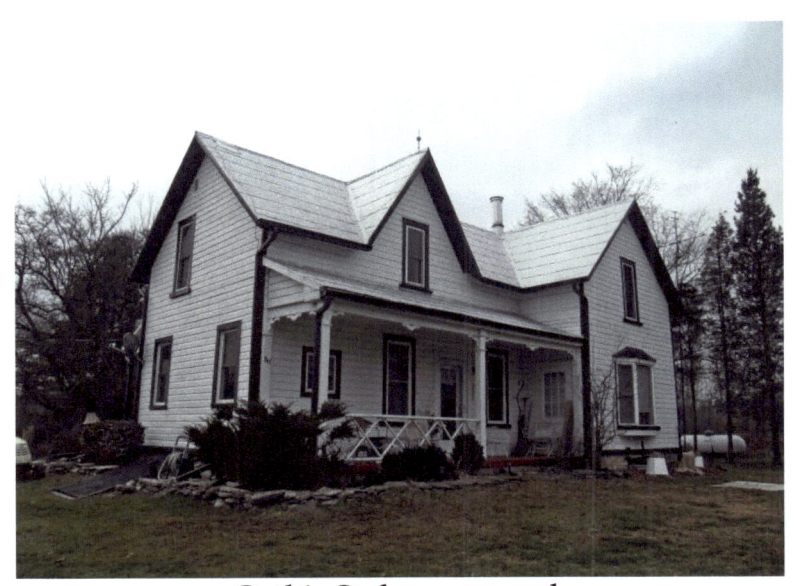

Gothic Style centre arch

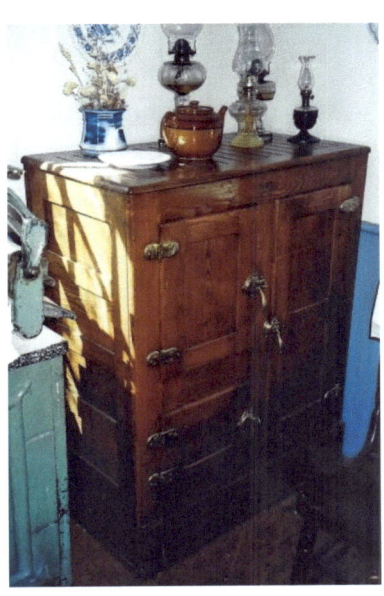

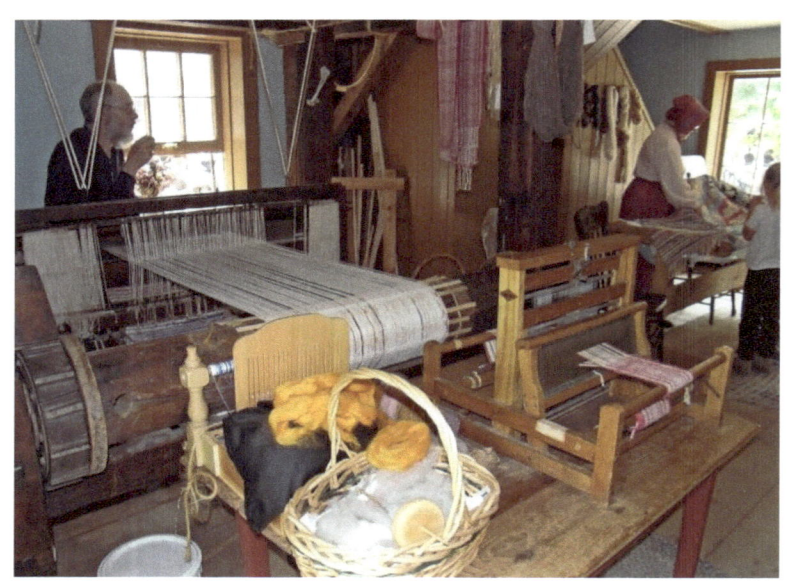

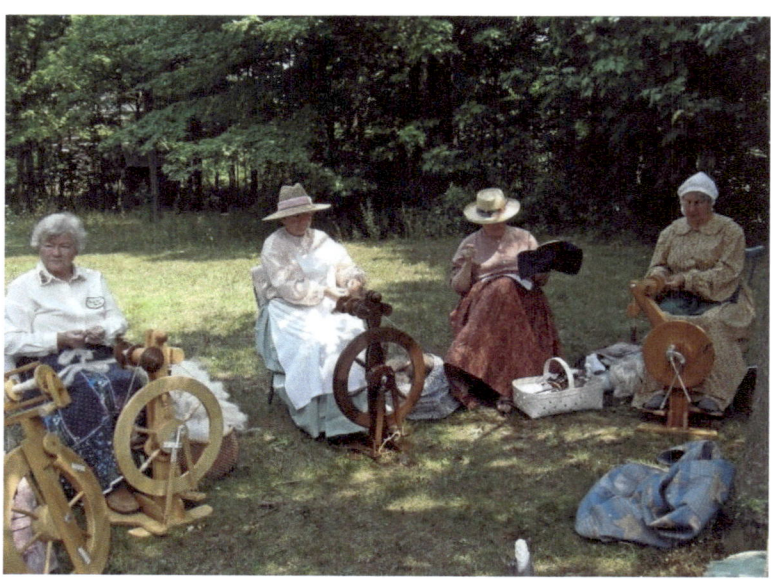

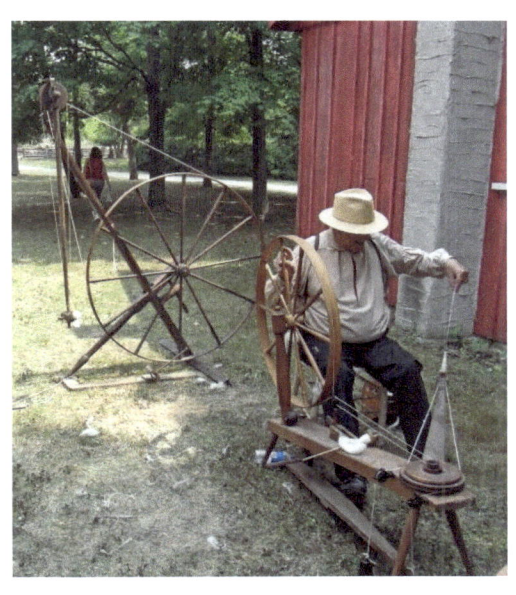

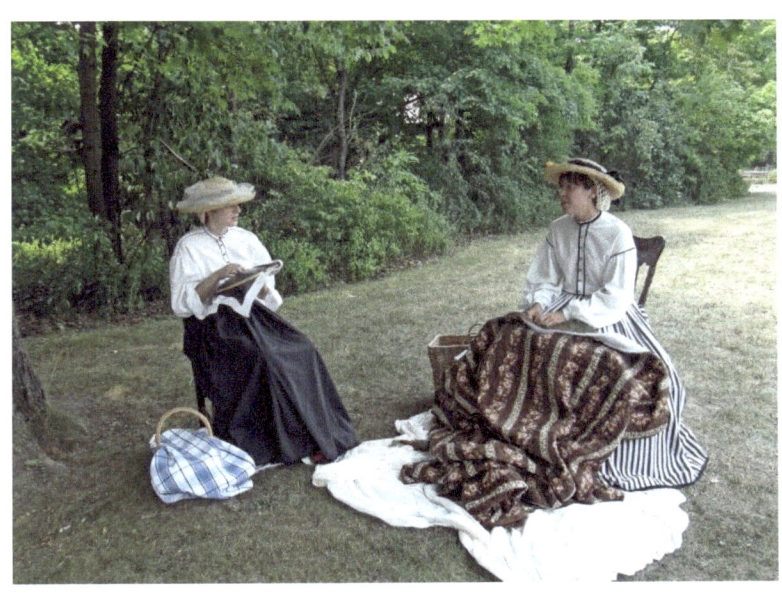

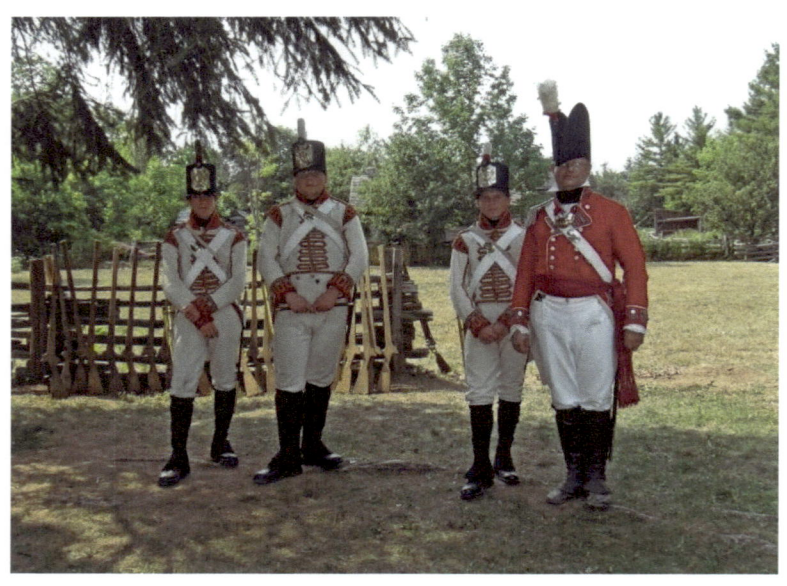

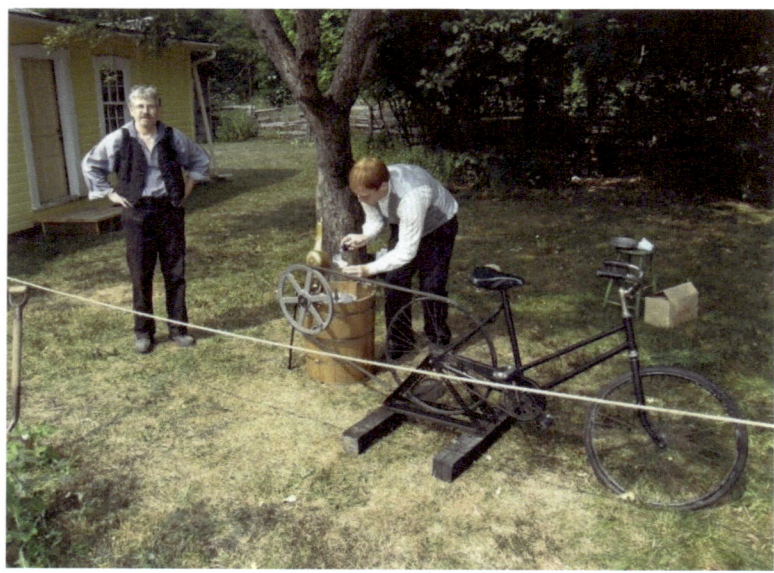

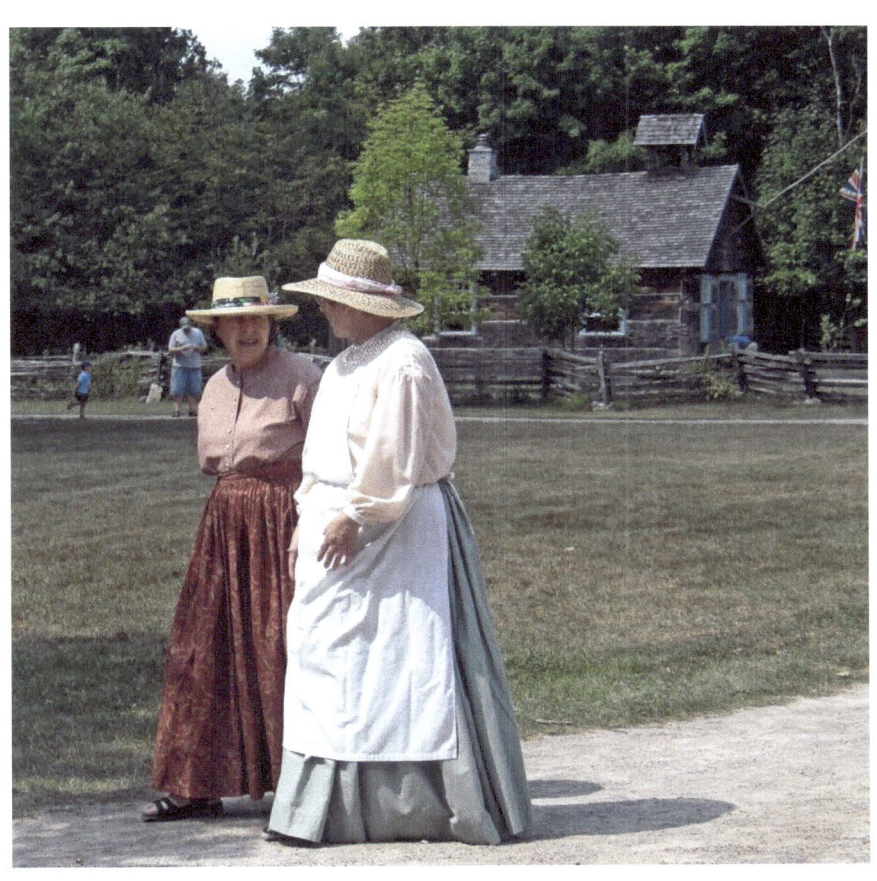

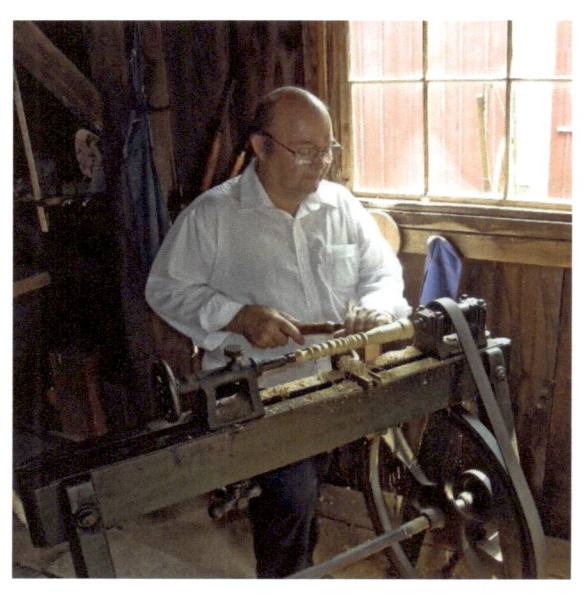

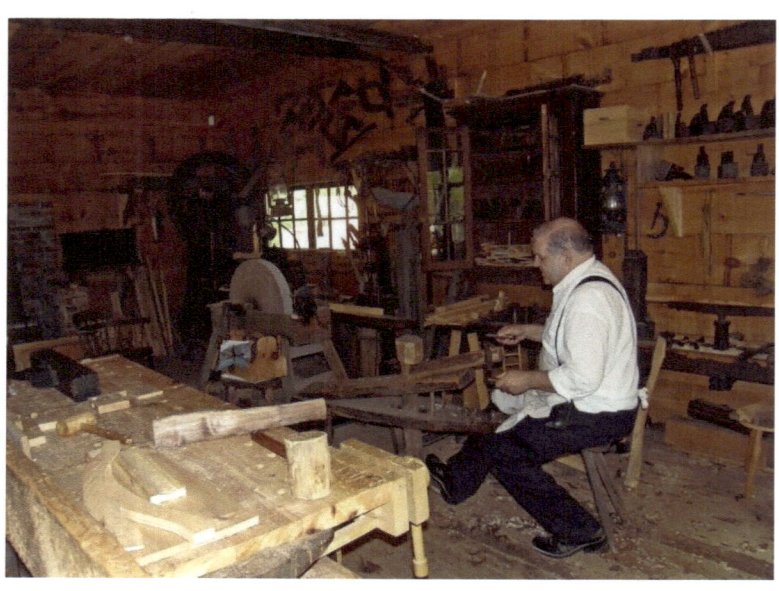

Anne of Green Gables Day

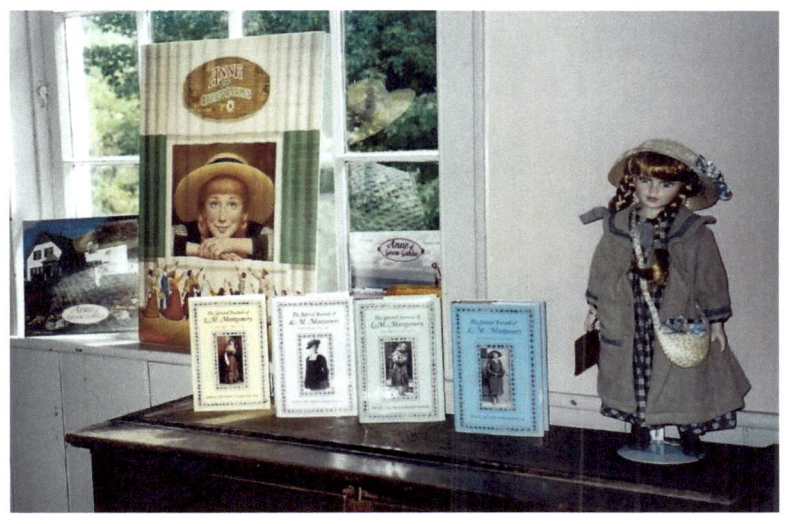

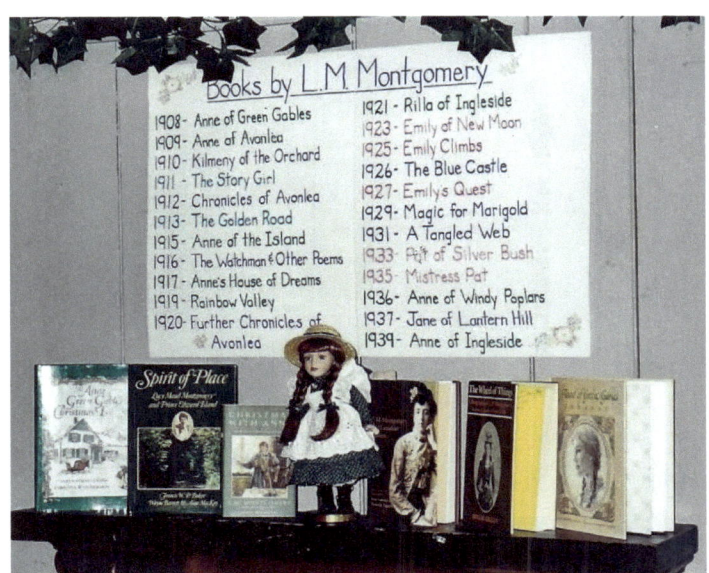

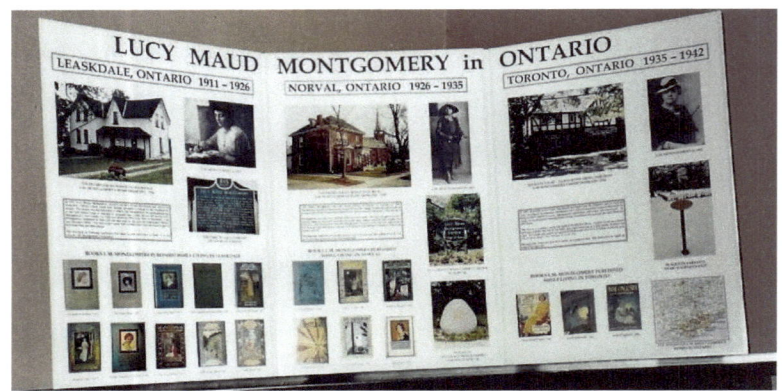

Lucy Maud Montgomery – author of Anne of Green Gables books

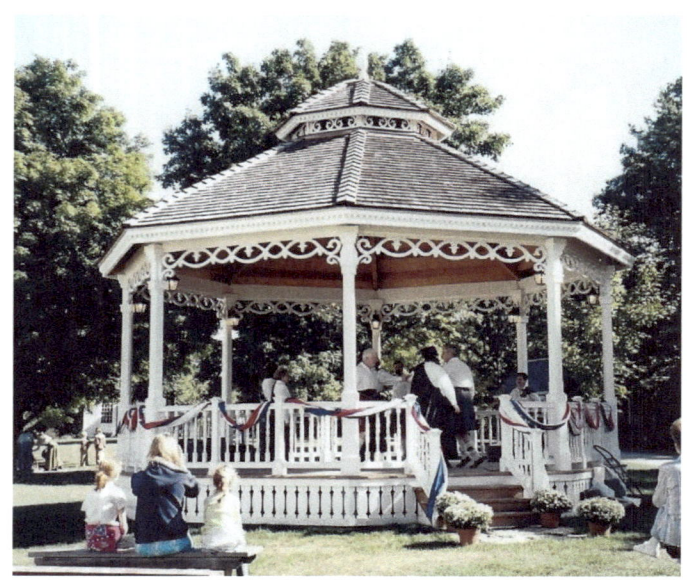

Square Dancing in the Bandstand

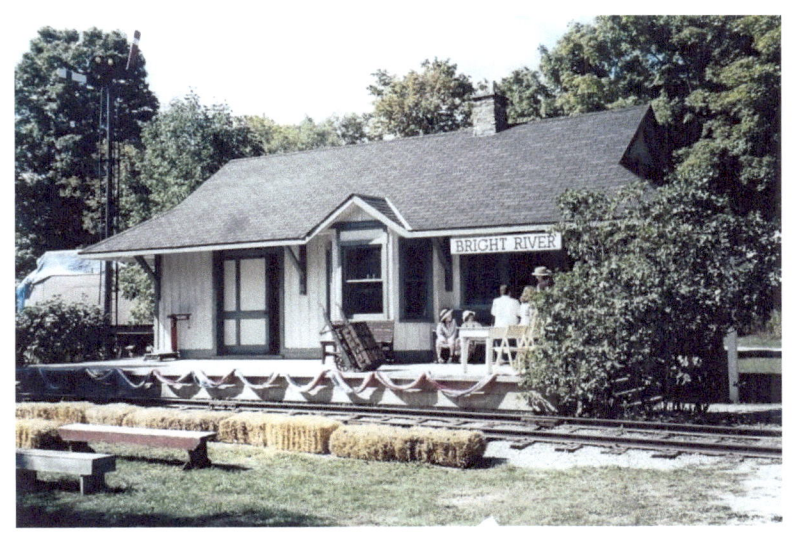

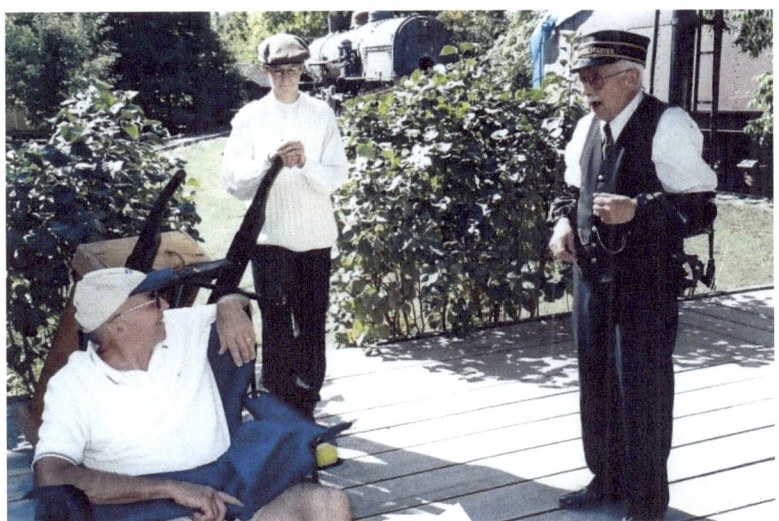

Station Master

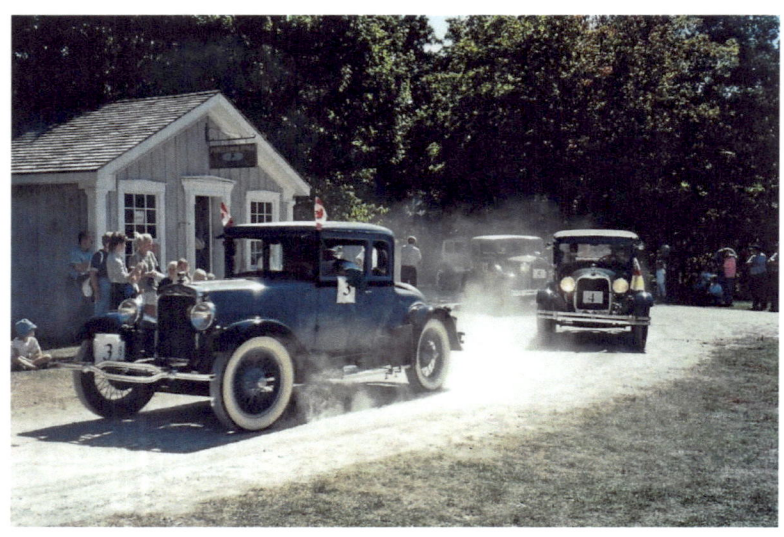

Antique Car Race

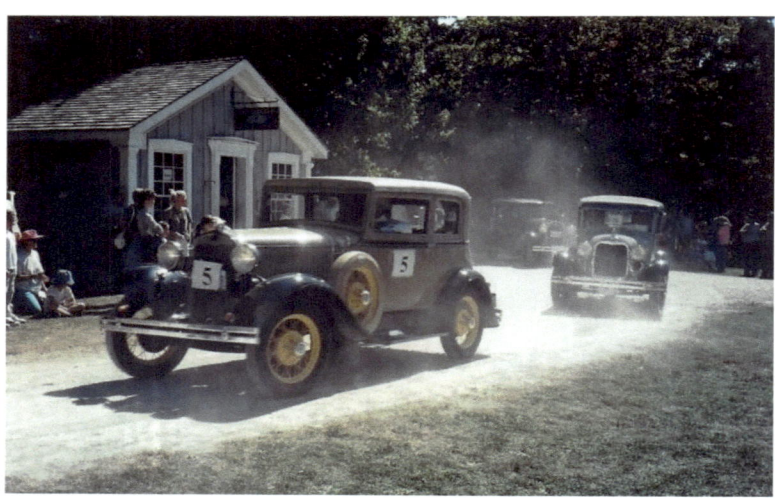

www.ingramcontent.com/pod-product-compliance
Lightning Source LLC
Chambersburg PA
CBHW040240220526
45473CB00001B/306